To Sarah

Co-Conspirator,

The Learning Revolution.

With appreciation for

your commitment and

support

Mark Engel

10/03

THE
EDUCATION REVOLUTION:
SPECTACULAR LEARNING
AT
LOWER COST

THE
EDUCATION REVOLUTION: SPECTACULAR LEARNING AT LOWER COST

MORTON EGOL

Wisdom Dynamics, LLC

FIRST EDITION

Library of Congress Cataloging-in-Publication data

Egol, Morton, 1941-
    The Education Revolution: Spectacular Learning
    At Lower Cost / Morton Egol

- 1st ed.

    p. cm.

    ISBN 0-9743193-0-9
    Includes Bibliography
    1. Education – Aims and objectives – United States. 2. Edu-
    cation Change – United States. 3. School Improvement Pro-
    gram – United States. 4. Government Productivity – United
    States. I. Title.

Control No. 2003108719

10 9 8 7 6 5 4 3 2 1

Printed in the United States of America on acid-free paper.

To Nancy,
Who lights up my life

ACKNOWLEDGEMENTS

This book and the prototype school described here would not have come to pass had it not been for the support and encouragement that I received from my partners at Arthur Andersen for the Firm's "School of the Future" program, which I led for 10 years. Foremost among them were Robert F. Kelley, Thomas B. Kelly, and Richard L. Measelle.

Michael Doyle, a master facilitator and strategic planning consultant, aided my planning and facilitated the community visioning process that resulted in strong support to establish the Community Learning Center in Alameda, California in 1996.

Ed Ward, a master facilitator and strategic planning consultant, has been of invaluable assistance to me in supporting the planning and assessment process at the Alameda Community Learning Center from 1997 to 2003 and in assisting me in conducting the four global conferences on "Learning for the 21st Century."

The trailblazing work of Daniel Greenberg in founding the democratically based Sudbury Valley School over 30 years ago, in Framingham, Massachusetts, and the many hours of conversation I had with him, provided inspiration and crucial insights about the importance of learners having an equal voice and vote in all decisions that affect them.

"If a nation expects to be ignorant and free, in a state of civilization, it expects what never was and never will be."
Thomas Jefferson, 1816

TABLE OF CONTENTS

PREFACE

This is a book about an educational revolution we need in order to sustain our freedom and quality of life. But it is a revolution not yet begun. In fact, today's education reforms and those of recent decades are taking us in the wrong direction.

These attempted reforms do not recognize the dramatic changes that are occurring as the world economy shifts from the dumbed-down, assembly-line worker of the Industrial Age to the empowered "knowledge worker" of the Information Age.

Rather than focus on redesigning the education system as a whole, reformers have attempted to tweak certain aspects of the system, such as by reducing class size or increasing the frequency of testing. These changes do not even begin to deal with the welter of systemic problems in our educational system. Instead, they further complicate matters and only make the situation worse.

The fundamental truth is that the traditional, Industrial-Age model of education is obsolete. A completely different education system is required in order to meet the needs of a new era. Instead of teaching passive "students," we need to create self-directed, lifelong "learners" who are capable of designing their own individual pathways to success.

The education system advocated in this book would abolish age-based groupings of students in individual classrooms, teacher-taught lessons, year-end tests, and virtually every other feature of today's schools. Through this new approach, the unintended consequences created by such traditional, authoritarian practices – passive students, high failure rates, and the crushing out of students' natural love for learning – would be solved.

The new system would empower learners (and teachers) to be self-directed giving them a voice in all decisions affecting them. It would provide them with the community linkages they need in order to understand how the world works. And it would enable them to perform meaningful, impactful work.

Self-directed learning, a cornerstone of the new education system, builds upon strengths and supports each individual's quest to fulfill his or her potential. It facilitates equal opportunity because it recognizes that every child's situation and capabilities are unique. Tragically and unfairly, the traditional system ignores such differences.

The level of educational quality that results from self-directed learning assures relevance, responsiveness, and fairness. It also costs less. Annual per-pupil expenditures for this new education system would be $5,940, compared to an average $7,520 for the 2002 school year, a reduction of approximately 20%. When fully implemented at the elementary and secondary-school level, the new system would produce annual savings of some $75 billion, which would permit salary increases for deserving teachers – along with reductions in taxes.

Larger economic advantages would also accrue. Students' greatly enhanced ability to learn under the new system would lead to their entering the workforce earlier, saving on college tuition, and increasing their productivity as workers. In the broadest sense, this approach to education would promote increased social cohesion, strengthen our political democracy, and enhance our overall quality of life.

The new education system I am describing is possible today. In September 1996, a school I helped found in Alameda, California, opened its doors to 150 multi-age, self-directed learners, ages 12-18, along with a team of five facilitators. The school's performance has exceeded expectations on a variety of measures. In 2002, in order to facilitate its further development, the school became a charter school.

This book lays out a vision and implementation strategy for the new education system. It includes a description of a day in the life of two learners and a facilitator. And it raises a call to action for political leaders and the citizenry, especially parents, teachers, philanthropists, and the business community. The appendices contain tools for planning a community visioning process and for preparing a charter school application.

For those who wish to deepen their understanding of the systems thinking perspective that underlies this new approach to education, the appendices also include a step-by-step build-up of a causal loop diagram showing how the new system creates a learning community with successful self-directed learners and how the system can sustain itself.

Morton Egol, August 2003

PART I: THE NEW LEARNING PARADIGM

The Challenge

Society and the nature of work are undergoing revolutionary changes in the Information Age. However, our schools cling to the practices of a bygone era and are thus becoming less and less relevant every day. Correcting the schools' individual deficiencies, or reforming the current system, which was designed for the Industrial Age, are inadequate responses to the change that has been thrust upon us. Reforming the current system would leave us with a perfect system for the Industrial Age, but the wrong system for today. Instead, we must totally redesign and transform education to meet the imperatives of a new era, in which mankind's total knowledge base is expanding exponentially and at a dizzying speed.

The shift required of us is a radical one. The basic structure of schooling – an authoritative teacher transmitting information piecemeal to a class of passive students – has not changed for centuries. As a result, the magnitude of change now required of today's schools is comparable to the shift from the horse and buggy to the automobile, and from the factory to the virtual workplace. By contrast, current efforts to improve the traditional education system amount to "more of the same." Indeed, the so-called "changes" being made in the name of reform only serve to reinforce the status quo and actually make matters worse. They will not achieve the purpose of preparing students to be self-reliant and effective citizens in a rapidly changing environment.

The trend toward a greater federal role in education is also going in the wrong direction. It reduces local control and complicates management and school governance at a time when localities should be designing new systems that empower learners, parents, and teachers to meet individual needs and to practice democracy at a grass roots level. The practice of citizenship, an important justification for the public schools, is rarely included in the debate about the condition of education.

The traditional education system is not delivering on its promise to maximize the opportunities for learning. This is not merely a matter of unequal resources and unequal access to better performing schools. The education system itself guarantees failure for some students by requiring all to learn the same things in the same way at the same rate, despite individual differences among students. And the pressures and humiliation created by testing and ranking crushes out love of learning and turns students off to schooling at an early age.

A substantial majority of parents believe that the schools their own children attend are performing adequately, and that the problem lies with someone else's school, largely those in the inner cities. However, essentially *all* schools are out of step with the times.

All children must be free to develop to their full potential and to master the skills that will make them self-reliant adults and effective citizens. This will require a quality and productivity breakthrough to a new system based on the natural love of learning – which is the foundation for lifelong learning.

What is required to achieve this breakthrough is a fundamentally different process for teaching and learning. To begin the transformational process, we need an imaginative and inspiring vision for the future of education.

Understanding the Revolution that is the Information Age

To design schools fit for the Information Age, we need to understand what has fundamentally changed. We need a shared understanding of the new ways of thinking, learning, working, and organizing that are emerging in this new era.

The Information Age does not simply mean a computer on every desk, nor everyone hooked up to the Internet. Instead, change itself has changed.

The accelerating pace of change has created a dilemma. By the time a strategy is formulated for any given situation, the situation has changed.

With an environment in such constant flux, reactive, linear thinking is inadequately robust, as are mechanistic ways of working and organizing. The brains at the top of hierarchical organizations cannot know enough, fast enough, to assign work through a command-and-control process.

In the world of work, leaders are trying to keep up by eliminating layers of middle management, harnessing the brainpower of entire organizations, and encouraging the formation of networks comprised of line personnel. Members of empowered teams increasingly participate in shared decision making.

But thus far, the empowerment process has been limited due to the lack of tools and skills that would enable these cross-functional teams to see the consequences of alternative courses of action on the organization as a whole. Genuine empowerment, therefore, is rare.

To support shared decision making, we need to utilize the tools of systems thinking and computer modeling. We solve the dilemma created by accelerating change by anticipating possibilities and adopting strategies that are robust against plausible scenarios. We cannot predict the future, but we can design an ideal future based on what is possible today. In doing so, we stay ahead of the change curve.

The shift from reactive thinking and a control model of dumbed-down, machine-like work, to the application of systems thinking by empowered teams, which enables an organization to anticipate all possibilities and simulate their consequences for the whole entity, is as revolutionary as was the division of labor to the Industrial Age.

Increasingly, systems thinking and associated simulation tools will allow organizations to validate their assumptions and strategies while increasing efficiencies through practice – much as pilots are trained by using flight simulators. In fact, as with piloting a plane, learning through real-world experience alone will prove too risky in a fast-changing world. To enhance their margin of safety, organizations' "experience" – their basis for decision making – will of necessity come to include practice and playing in virtual, simulated worlds. Beyond individual learning, organizations, too, must learn how to learn.

Why Traditional Schools are Wrong for the Information Age

Obviously, not all of these tools are consistently deployed in the work environment. Yet they will inevitably be deployed. And the continually adaptive thought processes they require will lead, in turn, to the new model for education proposed in this book.

An economy based on brainpower and a political system based on an informed citizenry requires an education system in which all succeed at learning at a much higher level, including mastery of thinking skills and lifelong learning skills. The poor learning habits inculcated by today's schools will need to be undone for today's students – and prevented for tomorrow's students. Consider these key issues that, among others, need to be addressed:

- The *theory of education* adhered to by today's schools views knowledge, in the form of imposed curricula, as a thing to be rigidly transferred by teacher to student (instead of created by the learner through purposeful work). This theory is not valid. The ever-quickening pace of knowledge development and its subsequent rapid obsolescence means that knowing a finite set of answers is not sufficient. In this increasingly complex world, there are always more questions than answers. No one can know enough.

- Nonetheless, in today's schools, students are expected to put aside their all-important natural curiosity and learn whatever the teacher or prescribed curriculum requires for any given day. The *passive role* thus assigned to the student is not conducive to genuine learning. Consequently, most of what is taught is forgotten soon after testing. Children learn best from immersion in work that they *choose* to do – because they can see relevance in it and can construct meaning from it.

- Another factor in the schools' obsolescence and irrelevance is the factory-like, assembly-line *structure* of schools. Under such a system, students are moved along without regard to individual differences, and those who can achieve much more than what is deemed standard go unchallenged. The teacher-centered classroom structure does not allow for any significant improvement in productivity. The teacher is typically consigned to a classroom with 15 to 40 students of the same age, who are isolated from other groups of students and required to follow standard curricula. Adhering to this structure actually locks in negative productivity, as the schools' costs rise each year while the amount of teaching and learning they impart remains essentially static.

- The schools' system of *evaluation* is also both invalid and counterproductive in its impact. In the existing system, students compete for grades and are ranked by "As" and "Fs," a distinction that by itself guarantees a significant failure rate. Moreover, the mere prospect of achieving only an average or failing performance, along with the pressure to perform, suppresses the natural love of learning and creates mental dropouts by the 3rd or 4th grade. For most students, school becomes an onerous place.

Many believe that smaller class size is the answer to these issues. However, despite countless studies on the effects of reducing class size, there is no consensus in these studies. At best, the beneficial effects are thought to be modest and confined to the early primary grades. We can see this in actual results, since there has been a decline in average class size in recent decades without improvement in student performance. Even if public schools were to reduce class size to 12-15 children, i.e., to the level of many private schools, there would be, at best, only minor improvements in student learning, but at a huge increase in cost. Reducing class size is simply more of the same, a simplistic approach to a very complex situation.

From Teachers-Teaching to Learners-Learning

Solutions to these inadequacies will not be found by tinkering with parts of the traditional model. What is indicated is fundamental change in order to create a relevant system with which to attain the quality and productivity breakthroughs necessary to achieve the learning requirements of the Information Age.

Consider the needs of today's learners. Addressing today's complex, multifaceted problems requires students to learn and think creatively. They require learners to develop the means for accessing each other's knowledge so as to take advantage of the full expertise and perspectives of the team. Addressing today's problems also requires enhanced social skills and the assumption of personal responsibility for one's learning. And it requires educators – and educational institutions – to *themselves* be model learners, i.e., continuously learning new things, anticipating new possibilities, restructuring themselves, and adapting to new circumstances as they arise.

The current static, stratified system simply cannot enable students to cope with the complexity of today's problems, the accelerating pace of change, and the new realities of the Information Age. What is required is a fundamental departure from the now-prevalent "teachers-teaching" education model to a "learners-learning" model.

In fact, there is a real-world example of this learner-centered model of education. It has been in place in Alameda, California, for better than six years. And the experience of its learners and staff provides an opportunity to glimpse the shape of the future of education – in the approach known as a Community Learning Center (CLC).

The new "learners-learning" model, as practiced in the CLC, draws its foundation from constructivist principles found in modern cognitive science, which is referred to as "Brain-Based Learning." Cognitive science reveals that learning is not achieved passively, but through an active process, wherein learners make meaning out of their work and experiences, applying information and ideas to create knowledge. According to constructivist principles, learning is best undertaken by self-directed learners who exercise their freedom and curiosity to explore areas of interest. At the CLC, these learners develop to their full potential as they customize their own education in ways that foster self-reliance and creativity, while also participating with others to develop skills of collaboration and democratic decision making. These methods can include discovery, meaning-making, and immersion in purposeful work.

In a learners-learning model, teachers do not cover a preset curriculum. Instead, the curriculum is "discovered" through self-direction, in which learners – with a facilitator's support and counsel – individually assume responsibility for their own education. Being self-directed provides the best motivation for nurturing the habit of lifelong learning.

The implications of this view of education are profound. It underscores that the learner should be part of a community of equals, should be afforded dignity and respect, and should be trusted to freely pursue his or her own goals and schedules. This approach respects the individual freedom and dignity of the learner and builds upon the learner's strengths, passionate interests and natural curiosity.   With this shift comes the recognition that learning is a process of constructing meaning ("meaning-making"), rather than one of "being taught" – passively internalizing knowledge.

The contrast with the existing system of schooling is stark. The current education system withholds trust, robs children of their freedom, and does not treat them as individuals. Under this prison-like form of education, the learner has no rights and is tightly controlled within the classroom setting. The system teaches to a mythical "average" student and thus fosters conformity and mediocrity. This runs counter to the values of individualism, creativity, and entrepreneurialism.

Self-directed, collaborative learning in a multi-age setting is an antidote to failure. At the CLC, unique styles of learning are accommodated and learners are allowed to tailor the pace at which they accomplish their own goals. The collaborative learning environment provides a "scaffolding" – a broad-based, multi-age framework that enables students to benefit from the advanced knowledge of more experienced students. It also includes a wide array of learning approaches, permitting the learners to choose or to build upon techniques that are of interest and that work best for them. Both elements – multi-*age* and multi-*discipline* – represent a fundamental and necessary change from the lockstep grade structure, which forces everyone to absorb the same things at the same rate. The issue of holding back or advancing a child under the rationale of "social promotion" does not even come up in a self-directed system.

Such a system is analogous to the one-room schoolhouse of the American frontier, which typically accommodated students of varying ages and talents, and where teachers relied on students to teach themselves and help each other learn. It also mirrors the kind of workplace that has been emerging in the Information Age, in which, as we have noted, companies of empowered, cross-functional teams seek to become "learning organizations."

We can sum up by saying, then, that spectacular increases in student learning will be possible only when the schools shift to a system that is rooted in discovery-based, self-directed learning, and linked to involvement in purposeful work.

Facilitation: The Teacher's New Role

In the self-directed approach that is represented by the CLC, approximately 150 learners are enrolled for at least six years. The CLC is staffed by a team of five adults, with varied experience and diverse subject-matter competencies, who are skilled in the facilitation of self-directed learning.

At the CLC, facilitators spend substantially all of their time directly interacting with learners, and they get to know each one very well. In such an environment, problems do not go undetected (as they do in the current system until end-of-term testing). Instead, they are quickly addressed, both individually and through the group, through peer feedback, requests for assistance, or observations by a facilitator.

CLCs enable continuous productivity improvement, self-management, and enhanced accountability. The traditional role of school principal is transformed to that of facilitator team leader – directly in contact with both the learners and other facilitators. In this way, the best, most experienced learning resources remain in close contact with learners, while an entire layer of middle management and related cost is removed.

The learner-centered CLCs offer enormous opportunities for improving the productivity and contributions of the facilitators. Instead of teaching the same thing year-in and year-out, facilitators coach individual learners and are models for life-long learning. Working in teams, they not only support the learners with regard to their self-directed goals, but they also assist in the design, development, and operation of the learning environment and its governance structure. In addition, facilitators spend significant time outside of the learning center with internship sponsors, mentors, parents, and alliance partners.

The team approach to facilitation assures continuous professional development of facilitators and strengthens accountability, since no team of facilitators will tolerate a member who does not respond to suggestions for improvement. And learners, who have a number of facilitators to approach for help, will not be stuck with a "bad" teacher, either.

In tandem with this team approach, each of the self-directed learners (and the facilitator-model learners), will pursue their own stretch learning goals – reaching beyond the next level of competence towards a vision of complete mastery. As with the "invisible hand" of the great 18th century philosopher and economist Adam Smith, everyone's effort to fulfill his or her own clearly defined, individual learning objectives will inevitably result in an optimal learning environment – one in which learners and their facilitators respond to the demand for specific learning goals. Individuals and self-organizing teams will collaborate toward common objectives, informing learners' own plans as well as the overall plans for the CLC. Out of the chaos of individual choice, order will emerge.

Continuous feedback and self-referencing among learners and facilitators will create a living system, a self-organizing learning community. The CLC, comprised of self-directed learners, will continually improve and restructure itself to meet the ever changing needs of each learner and the community.

From Students Doing Time to Learners Using Time

Time, of course, is the ultimate resource; and the heart of self-directed learning is the freedom and responsibility of learners to design their own timetables. This freedom is where cognitive science converges with modern organizational theory and political democracy. Instead of a highly controlled, prison-like setting, in which learners move from class to class in accordance with a bell schedule, learners at the CLC will be responsible for how they spend their time. Only by being in charge of themselves, will they learn how to be self-reliant and to allocate their time productively.

The fragmentation of time in the traditional education system, i.e., the division of the schooling process into courses and semesters, and the school day into 45-60 minute periods, is destructive of quality, efficiency, and effectiveness. This is because (a) the breadth and depth of inquiry is greatly restricted, (b) learners who change schools during the school year or who miss days due to illness may not be able to catch up, and (c) putting in "seat time" is required to obtain the credential, even if the learner has mastered the requirements.

Self-directed learning ends the fragmentation of time and "dis-solves" all of these problems plus many more deficiencies. Most importantly, it reinforces love of learning and allows learners to exercise freedom and responsibility to spend their own time as they see fit.

Free to design their own learning programs and free of the bell schedule that fragments learning into hourly bites, learners will be able to immerse themselves in areas of passionate interest and to build on their strengths. By building up their "knowledge capital," they will be able to help others to acquire knowledge and learn similar skills. Freed from the bell schedule, learners will be continuously available to each other for cooperative learning and for accessing each other's knowledge.

From Standard Curricula to Freedom-to-Think and Learning-to-Learn

Leaders in traditional schools recognize that modern schools must go beyond the traditional basics of reading, writing and arithmetic. They also recognize that modern cognitive science demands that learners construct meaning in their work. They therefore espouse the injection of "critical thinking skills" into the curricula and initiate such techniques as "project-based learning" and "interdisciplinary learning" to create opportunities for more interesting, personalized learning and to better cover traditional subject matter. However, the manner in which they act on this insight is far from perfect, constrained by an inherently inadequate system.

These efforts to inject critical thinking skills merely fit new learning theory into old curricula, rather than redesigning the process of learning and the traditional curricula to fit the new learning theory. The limitations of this approach will become ever more apparent over time, as knowledge's exponential expansion makes it ever clearer that traditional schools cannot cover all important domains of knowledge.

Schooling must shift to self-directed learners with the lifelong skills of Learning-to-Think and Learning-to-Learn that will enable them to acquire a wider range of knowledge as they need it. Chief among these skills are:

- Strategic Reading and Speed Reading
- Effective Writing
- Research
- Note-Taking
- Effective Presentations
- Listening
- Dialogue
- Logic
- Problem-Solving and Problem Dis-Solving
- Creative Thinking
- Systems Thinking and System Dynamics
- Computer Programming, Modeling and Simulation
- Decision making
- Facilitation (of learning, dialogue, etc.)
- Teamwork and Collaborative Learning
- Conflict Resolution
- Self-Assessment and Organizational Assessment
- Work Organization
- Time Management
- Total Quality Management

Most of what is now "learned" in school is forgotten soon after the final exam. However, thinking and learning skills are enduring and will always be relevant.

Following is a brief description of certain of the above thinking and learning-to-learn skills.

Strategic Reading and Speed-Reading is about efficiency, effectiveness, and increasing both comprehension and understanding; It is also about how to extract information rapidly through selection, preview, scanning, assessing the structure of the material, summarizing key ideas, and reflection.

Effective Presentations is about communications, i.e., conveying information to others in a way that engages and persuades them to provide feedback, share beliefs or take action. It includes the art of influencing others to share information and to enter into cooperative learning arrangements.

Dialogue is the art of collective inquiry. It recognizes that learning is a social and interactive process that seeks shared understanding and solutions, not winning in discussions, debates or arguments.

Systems Thinking or System Dynamics will become part of the "new basics" under the new system of learning, as the Information Age unfolds. It is about understanding causality and complexity. Activities in systems thinking include graphically documenting interactions of key variables, along with computer modeling of issues, organizational dynamics and behavior in ways that permit learning and the synthesis of ideas.

Total Quality Management is the art and science of continuous improvement by organizing systems and work activities in order to achieve objectives without error. It provides tools and techniques for use by empowered teams.

Development of freedom-to-think and learning-to-learn skills is a direct result of practicing self-directed learning. In a self-directed program, learners may utilize technical publications and books, participate in seminars at the CLC or local community colleges, and apply learned techniques in apprenticeships and internships. They also may practice their skills by serving as faculty for thinking and learning-to-learn seminars conducted for K-5 groups and for adult after-school programs.

In a learner-centered education system, mastery of thinking and learning-to-learn skills would be reinforced through their application in the continuous design and development of strategies, programs, and tools for use in the CLC. Learners would actually gain "certification" to serve as facilitators in seminars conducted at the CLC.

Learners would also self-assess their needs in various content areas, such as history, literature, and biology, and design their learning-to-learn programs with those content areas in mind. Thus, traditional curricula would be learned as a by-product of developing thinking and learning-to-learn skills.

For example, learners might decide to develop their presentation and speed-reading skills. They could do this in a way that would also enhance their awareness of literature. They might design and conduct seminars on reading and effective presentations skills. As part of this activity, each learner would select randomly from 200 of the world's greatest works of literature and then prepare a short speech or presentation. These would be critiqued by an audience of other learners. Under this approach, learners would acquire such skills as effective presentation, listening, providing feedback, and speed-reading, while also being exposed to much of the world's great literature. They would be self-motivated to read many of the great works of literature at their leisure.

Today's students have very limited exposure to learning-to-learn skills and a fairly narrow exposure to great literature, since they typically read in lockstep from the same selections – selections that are ultimately determined by the teacher or by the standard curriculum.

Another example is in the application of math and writing while learning systems thinking, computer modeling and simulation skills. Using computer modeling and simulations, learners might decide to devise alternative strategies for solving problems facing the CLC, the community, or even the nation. Constructing the models would require learners to develop their math skills, in order to formulate the interactions of complex variables. It would require them to reinforce their writing skills in order to document assumptions. And it would also require them to gain broader knowledge in the social sciences. Learners might take the initiative further by creating "virtual" learning environments and then make them available on their CLC's Website for use by the entire community. Many in the community would come to view the CLC as a knowledge-creating resource and engage the CLC in a variety of useful projects.

Learners Helping Others, Engaged in Purposeful Work

Another important benefit of a learner-centered education system is the inherently greater meaningfulness of the educational experience, to both the learner and society. While learning should be a fun and joyful experience, it must be meaningful to the learner. It must lead to a sense of genuine accomplishment, not merely to a high grade point average. This is where the traditional system is most deficient.

The weakness is most apparent with regard to the treatment of middle school students. At ages 12-14, the time when youngsters are struggling to define themselves and are possessed of enormous energy, the traditional system treats them as victims of hormonal imbalance, incapable of doing important work. Instead of providing them with freedom to channel their energies into creative, purposeful work that is valuable to themselves and to the community, they are deprived of any such rites of passage into adulthood. The result is rebellion against imposed structure, which reinforces the opinion that they are incapable of being trusted to take charge of their learning and of performing important work. This is a vicious cycle.

Low expectations are self-fulfilling. But so are high expectations. Empowering learners to be self-directed signals high expectations and dis-solves this problem. It provides all learners with the opportunity to develop naturally, while also providing channels for purposeful work. The multi-age structure in a CLC provides a natural "scaffolding" – a framework for both viewing and scaling higher levels of achievement. Such a structure allows younger learners to gauge the levels of achievement that they wish to attain and to select role models from among more experienced learners, including facilitators. And the older learners obtain the satisfaction that comes from helping others and from being role models.

The meaningfulness of learning extends into actual management of the CLC. Learners are responsible for the design, development, and operation of the learning environment and carry out all of the functions, both academic and administrative, at the CLC. They also form clubs and corporations to carry out their vision.

On the academic level, self-directed learners, grounded in cognitive science and the art of facilitation, assist less experienced learners. They may also lead seminars on a variety of learning skills during regular school hours and serve on the faculty for adult learning programs conducted after regular school hours. By facilitating the learning of others and by applying their knowledge as facilitators in the performance of purposeful work, learners reinforce their learning-to-learn skills and develop excellent habits that prepare them for the workplace.

On the administrative level, learners participate in carrying out a variety of CLC functions, including planning, budgeting, accounting, purchasing, information systems maintenance, and performance measurement.

Learners conduct research into best practices in all areas of importance to the center's vision and long-term plans. Learners also participate developing learning methods and tools and in executing strategies for the success of the center.

By empowering learners with the responsibility for their own learning and for the success of the CLC, schoolwork becomes truly purposeful. In doing so, it fully brings to life the well-known educational creed of "learning by doing."

PART II: LINKS TO THE COMMUNITY

As these examples of learner activity demonstrate, one precept of the learner-centered approach to education is service to others, starting with other students and the CLC itself. Apprenticing CLC learners to the schools would equip them with the skills to function effectively in business, not-for-profit, and governmental organizations. However, the impact of the CLC model extends beyond the school into the community – and this can take a number of significant forms.

Bridging Schoolwork to the "Real World" through Internships

Linking learning to the real world through internships would make schoolwork more meaningful and expose learners to multiple career paths. It would also create opportunities for mentoring relationships to form. Facilitators who arrange these internships could choose to participate in the internship programs as well, bringing their skills to bear in a variety of ways, such as designing training programs for the sponsoring organizations. This would greatly enhance their standing and their ability to exercise leadership in the design of CLC strategies and programs.

Internships would include working off-site at the sponsoring organizations' facilities, as well as working "virtually," through computer networks and on-line conferencing. Formal feedback on learner performance and capabilities would be much more valuable for learners and facilitators than scores on paper-and-pencil tests.

Advanced learners would participate in 5-10 different internship programs during their tenure at the CLC. In addition to broadening the experience of the learner, internships would dis-solve one of the greatest deficiencies of the current system. This is one in which students complete their schooling but have no idea of what career to pursue and do not possess the knowledge or tools to effectively assess any options.

With their creative thinking abilities, learner-interns would be enormously valuable as workers to sponsoring organizations, which would financially contribute to the CLC based on the hours worked. Of much broader value, however, would be the experience and knowledge brought into the CLC, which would benefit all learners while ensuring that the CLC continues to remain relevant.

These internships would reinforce self-directed learning, but they would not be "required" programs. Learners would decide how best to prepare for the internships they do choose to apply for, and they would develop their learning plans accordingly. Learners who successfully complete internships would be an excellent source of information for other learners.

The social, political, and economic capital that would be created by learner-internships cannot be overestimated. Interns' exposure to the real world, their experiences of learning-by-observation, and their interaction with people in all walks of life would help to perpetuate our national values of self-reliance, diversity, capitalism, and democracy, while fostering deep understanding of the interplay of these values in real life.

Students as Stewards, Engaged in School Governance

In a multi-age, self-directed learning environment of 150 learners aged 12 to 18, approximately 25 learners graduate each year and 25 learners enter. A never-ending, "living system" thereby comes into existence – one in which learners are responsible for continually improving their learning community and for adopting policies and programs that will assure its continued relevance. In effect, students become stewards of the school.

As stewards, learners should be empowered to participate in all decisions that affect them. Beyond enhancing the learning process, this helps fulfill a primary purpose of schooling: to support democratic institutions and to produce effective citizens.

However, learners cannot be empowered if facilitators, in turn, are not genuinely empowered. Therefore, school boards and superintendents who oversee policy should delegate operating responsibility to CLCs, granting line-item budget authority within overall spending limits. Such site-based management authority would enable facilitators and learners to address strategic and day-to-day issues affecting the life of the center. In practice, to assure the right level of independence in this and in other areas, it may be necessary to establish the CLC as a charter school.

The CLC should be governed under the terms of a "Constitution" drawn up by an Assembly comprised of parents, learners, and facilitators. Weekly "School Meetings" patterned after New England town meetings and chaired by an elected learner would address all operating issues. Annual plans, line-item budgets, and evaluations of leadership performance would be ratified and acted upon by the School Meeting and the Assembly.

There should be no concern about a child under the age of eighteen having an equal vote with facilitators. Aside from the fact that all learners should be treated with dignity and should learn how to practice democracy at an early age, such empowerment will make learners more aware of the consequences of their decisions. They will fully recognize that the failure of the CLC would result in its closure, the return of learners to traditional schools, and the attendant loss of the educational benefits the CLC has provided. In addition, facilitators will actually gain authority, in the eyes of the learners, from having shown the respect and trust necessary to share responsibility with them.

The democratic governing principles applied in the CLC may seem too radical for some. They involve a fundamentally different attitude toward children than the one embodied in our current education system, which assumes that children are irresponsible and must be controlled. The fundamental insight that invalidates this attitude is that, in most cases, children are simply behaving in accordance with the low behavioral expectations that have been set for them and are "acting out" against the rigid structure imposed on them. This creates a vicious cycle of "control" that leads to misbehavior that leads to greater "control."

Discipline is an area where a learner-centered model would have tremendous beneficial impact. Under a CLC's constitution, a learner-elected Judicial Committee, i.e., a "court" following rules of due process, would be empowered to hear and adjudicate all complaints by learners against other learners. This committee would mete out justice in the form of required service, loss of privileges, and other appropriate sanctions. Because there is no authority figure leading the class who would be a target for rebellion, there will be little desire by learners to be disruptive. Also, the fact that each learner is empowered to bring charges in the Judicial Committee against any rule breaker should deter anyone from misbehaving. Most offenders would likely plead guilty before the Judicial Committee; they are being judged by their peers, not subject to reprimand by a teacher in a battle of wills that makes the offender the center of attention.

For all of these reasons, discipline would be much less of a problem in a multi-age, self-directed learning environment than it is in a traditional school. In this new paradigm, maintaining discipline, even for offenders, becomes a lesson in self-regulation, good citizenship, and participatory democracy.

The new education system, based on the principles of freedom and individual rights, proceeds from the assumption that if we treat children with respect and provide them with tools for their natural development, they will tend to behave in accordance with our heightened expectations. And if some don't, the group will judiciously act to maintain order and preserve group values.

Assessment as a Learning Process

In traditional schools, assessment is closely allied with discipline. Testing students is a method of controlling them by encouraging competition and instilling fear of failure. Standardized test results are used as a tool to establish accountability for teacher and administrator performance.

Standardized testing and final exams, taken for granted as a basic part of the traditional system, has many pernicious effects. For example, a student who falls short on only a single question may be required to retake an entire course under pain of failing to graduate. Also, test papers are frequently not returned to students to allow them to see which items were judged to be incorrect. Consequently, lowering of standards or "social promotion" frequently occurs. When students are treated in this manner, and humiliated by ranking, it is no wonder that many of them grow to hate school.

It is regrettable that the drive for better results has led to an increased emphasis on standardized testing, which accentuates the worst features of the traditional learning model and reduces the freedom of both students and teachers. Students are forced to compete for grades, which reduces the incentive to work cooperatively with other learners. Teachers tend to narrow the scope of instruction to the subject matter that is expected to be on the tests, and learners de-emphasize or ignore anything that does not count toward their grade. As a result, soon after the final test, learners promptly forget most of what they have "learned." But the bad habits of cramming, procrastination, and superficial learning persist and will someday have to be unlearned.

By contrast, in a system based on self-direction, the purpose of assessment is not to pass or fail students at the end of the year, but rather to enhance learning. Self-directed learning involves self-assessment, which is a critical element of learning-to-learn and taking responsibility for one's own education. Self-directed learners document their work on a routine basis, benchmark their performance, and develop portfolios as a basis for reflection and obtaining periodic feedback from peers, parents and facilitators. They also receive feedback from users of their services in connection with apprenticeships and internships. Self-directed learners periodically schedule demonstrations of mastery of their capabilities to facilitators and peers, replacing tests with creative celebrations of success, providing everyone with a learning experience.

Learners should take the initiative in designing and implementing the CLC's performance measurement system. They should likewise play a leading role in annually assessing progress toward fulfilling the center's long-term vision and operating goals. This internal reporting process should culminate in the preparation of an annual report to the community detailing accomplishments measured against all goals, while laying out plans for the ensuing year.

Although state and federal laws, colleges, and parents may require learners to take standardized tests, this should not pose an insurmountable barrier to transforming the education system. Self-directed learners who are responsible for designing their learning environment can be inventive in constructing programs and devising self-study tools that help them achieve their individual goals on standardized tests and college application exams. Over time, the advantages of the new education system and its self-assessment process will prevail. Standardized testing will decline in importance, and will eventually be abolished.

Technology for Self-Directed Learning, Networking, and Global Connectivity

Traditional schools are making large investments in computers and related technology. But rather than using technology's full potential to reinvent education, they are merely automating today's obsolete learning model through such programs as "distance learning." Instead of such add-ons, schools need to fully integrate technology into their curricula, much as it is now employed in the workplace to enable empowerment, shared decision making, and new ways of working.

Technology implies a great deal more than computers, printers, copying machines, and the Web. For example, a sophisticated video-recording studio is a valuable resource for producing films and Web-based materials, documenting performing arts productions, developing learning tools, and for creating self-assessment portfolios. Software tools can facilitate group dialogue, school projects, and school administration.

Technology also presents wonderful opportunities to enrich play, and, in the process, promote basic learning skills, such as teamwork, time management, interpersonal skills, computer skills, and strategic thinking. "Playing with ideas," a common expression describing the essence of creative, real-world work, is increasingly coming to mean, "Let's build a simulator and play-out all the alternatives that can be imagined."

At the CLC, technology can empower self-directed learners by allowing them to link with real-world practitioners engaged in important, purposeful work. For example, teams of learners may encounter community needs or problems they want to address, such as land-use development, traffic congestion, or affordable housing. They might do research and prepare computer simulation models to explore the relevant issues and formulate preliminary strategies. The computer-based tools and proposed solutions might then be provided to community leaders and others working on the same issues, leading to continuous interaction and participation all the way through to completion of a project. These tools also would be a valuable resource for learners' participation in virtual apprenticeships and internships.

Another example: learners might look into a broad issue such as global warming and construct Web-based tools to attract participation by others worldwide. Global projects utilizing the Internet present opportunities to learn world history, sociology, geography, and multiple languages through immersion in virtual communities.

Technology management, including network maintenance, presents a wonderful learning opportunity. After gaining suitable experience, the learners might start a related business, such as a tech support shop, to serve other schools and the broader needs of the community. Learners might also serve as faculty for adult technology tutorials offered after regular school hours.

Technology supports self-directed, self-paced learning, which can be a great force to promote equal opportunity, which is a key purpose of our education system. However, a "Digital Divide" has emerged to widen the opportunity gap between technology haves and have-nots. By transforming large traditional schools into small community learning centers that are accessible both days and evenings and are equipped with advanced technology, we take a giant step toward equal opportunity and relevant learning for all.

From Large "Egg-Crate" Schools to Small Community Learning Centers

Instead of large factory-like schools, which are out of touch with their student bodies, the new learner-centered system requires small, more intimate, neighborhood schools.

Limiting enrollment in CLCs to some 150 multi-age learners enables everyone to know one another and to continuously interact and access each other's knowledge. A town of 10,000 people would have approximately 15 CLCs instead of four elementary schools, two middle schools and one high school. Meanwhile, a city neighborhood would have several CLCs that collectively are located within walking distance of all homes in the area.

The small size and intimacy of the CLC also has a direct impact on learning and safety. The smaller size of a CLC means more of them can be built, and the proximity of the CLC to area residents allows easy access to the center's advanced technology during after-school hours. Proximity of a CLC to each learner's home also produces a special advantage in the inner city, where learners join gangs for protection because they have to pass through a number of gang territories on the way to high school. By reducing the distance students need to travel, we will generally minimize such issues.

CLCs also enable school districts to accommodate growth of student populations on a timely basis. Now, children must endure overcrowded classrooms or temporary trailer classrooms until demographics change sufficiently to justify additional school construction. CLCs also permit small localities to accommodate the needs of their entire population, whereas many small communities now find it necessary to send high school students to regional schools. CLCs can also better accommodate contractions in population, as their open structure makes them easy to transform in order to meet other purposes.

A typical CLC would have floor space of about 12,000 square feet, most of it comprising the Great Room, which would contain clusters of computers and work areas to support knowledge-creating activities of every variety. The perimeter of the area would include several conference rooms of various sizes, some equipped with specialty "groupware" to enhance collaborative work. A "biosphere" would serve as the center for work in the natural sciences. Music synthesizers would be located near the video-recording studio. All equipment would be on wheels to allow for creation of open space or a stage for performances and artistry of every type. A kitchen would be staffed completely by the learners, serving occasional tours of duty.

After a period of transition, in which traditional school hours would be observed, normal hours of the CLC would be 9 a.m. to 5 p.m. However, facilitators would provide coverage from 7 a.m. to 9 a.m. and 5 p.m. to 7 p.m., on a rotating basis, in order to accommodate learners who wished additional time in the CLC. During the evening hours, the CLC would be open for adult programs on such subjects as technology, systems thinking, and creative thinking. Volunteer learners would serve as facilitators, along with a supplemental group of adult facilitators.

Over time, the CLC would expand its program from five days a week to seven days a week, twelve months a year. At long last, the education system will transition from the farmer's calendar of the Agricultural Age to the ever-accessible resource that is needed in the Information Age.

Meanwhile, in a separate wing of the CLC, facilities for pre-kindergarten children, ages 3 to 5, will accommodate the day-care needs of parents, as well as the learning needs of the children (Day care without learning is not proper care.). This program would provide another opportunity for purposeful work by the older learners, who would work with staff and volunteer parents in the toddler section of the CLC.

CLCs as Learning Organizations with Local and Global Linkages

We have noted that the accelerating pace of change requires that every organization be a "learning organization," capable of anticipating change and adapting to change. In this sense, the successful CLC engages in a continuous process of assessing its own future and identifying the developmental options that are best suited to its purpose and capabilities.

At this CLC, all assumptions underlying the shared vision are periodically re-examined. Developments in the world of work and in cognitive science, along with various social factors, are continuously monitored and explored by learners and facilitators. Equally important, the assumptions regarding the attitudes and interests of learners, parents, facilitators, and other stakeholders are also reassessed. This process would make use of such techniques as learner and parent surveys, benchmarkings, and interviews.

Beyond such standard tools, CLCs would also benefit from the self-assessment tools made possible by systems thinking that are beginning to be employed by progressive organizations. Their evaluation and decision support processes can draw upon the latest concepts in accounting and performance assessment, such as Dynamic Scoring™ (a new accounting model created by the author of this book, based upon the principles of systems thinking and system dynamics). Dynamic Scoring does much more than measure inputs and outputs. It demonstrates how key success factors interact to create value, revealing the feedback structures and patterns of behavior that produce learning and results. The feedback structures are reflected in computer models and simulation tools used for scenario planning. Alternative strategies are tested and practiced before they are applied, reducing the organization's risk of failure and enhancing its capacity for effective innovation.

Learner participation in the assessment process is a logical extension of learner self-assessment and is good practice for the skills needed in the 21st century, including systems thinking, computer modeling, mathematics, shared dialogue, and shared decision making.

As a "learning organization," the successful CLC also would reach out to and conduct studies of other CLCs in order to benchmark its own performance and identify best practices. This would inevitably lead to the formation of joint projects and alliances that would leverage the capabilities of all the participating centers.

On a broad scale, CLCs in five or more different time zones throughout the world might link-up to undertake research and development projects or entrepreneurial ventures. By doing so they would be able to hand off their work to each other 24 hours of the day, seven days a week, and 360 days of the year. This would dramatically increase their productivity, while exposing learners to many cultures and enhancing their understanding of how the world works.

CLCs might also combine their skills and knowledge with those of other CLCs to address local or national issues, fostering improved relationships among diverse cultural, racial, and ethnic groups. This could be done through international "Learner Olympics" competitions, displays of learner accomplishment, establishment of entrepreneurial ventures, or sports leagues.

CLCs also might form relationships with colleges and universities for mutual advantage. For example, college students might participate in the CLCs as mentors, leading seminars on advanced topics of inquiry that go beyond the personal knowledge of local CLC facilitators. CLC learners might take selected courses at colleges or via Web-based interactive seminars and then lead seminars at the CLC. College students majoring in education might serve as facilitators in the CLC as part of their academic coursework and in fulfillment of their student-teaching requirements.

The CLC would leverage its learning through local and global linkages and alliances with other organizations, such as museums, research organizations, businesses, foundations, and community organizations.

Alumni, parents, and community members would develop a lifelong commitment to the CLC and would become actively involved in the life of the CLC. The CLC would be the catalyst for building a "learning community," a source of badly needed social cohesion.

From Higher Education to Lifelong Learning

As we transition to a knowledge-based economy, a majority of high-school graduates already go on to college, while a growing percentage of college graduates also obtain master's and doctorate degrees. However, as change accelerates and knowledge obsoletes itself, the traditional goal of such advanced study – the acquisition of a specific body of knowledge that will serve the student throughout a professional career – is becoming of increasingly limited value. The time devoted to this traditional model of formal "higher" education should therefore be reduced, rather than further extended into the years of adulthood.

In time, increased learner productivity from self-directed learning, lifelong learning skills, and internships will result in a shift from ever-increasing formal education, as it is conducted today, to more relevant learning conducted at CLCs. The results will include manifold societal benefits that are currently denied to students who are forced to extend their childhoods and delay their economic livelihoods. Visible evidence of these benefits will include adults' earlier entry into the workforce and an enhanced stream of younger entrepreneurs and empowered professionals.

Because their skill levels will be higher and because they will be better equipped to continue learning indefinitely, CLC graduates will likely enter the workforce at age 17-20, rather than at 22-25. Unleashing this stream of well-educated, capable, and flexible workers will enhance the nation's competitive position, provide for the health and retirement of the aging population, and substantially increase graduates' lifetime earnings potential.

The great universities will survive thanks to their well-established, specialized graduate and professional programs. But, over time, most four-year colleges will no longer continue to exist in their current form.

This shift to a new model will be facilitated by close linkages between CLCs and the world of work. As business organizations enter into school-to-work and internship programs with CLCs, they will realize significant improvements in productivity as well as savings in remediation and training costs. Eventually, today's fragmented education system of K-12, higher education, and business training will become a unified learning system. Networks of CLCs serving children and adults of all ages, linked to the world of work through internships, specialty training, self-directed on-line learning, and graduate schools will reduce the time required for formal schooling while offering the flexibility for lifelong learning.

PART III: BREAKTHROUGH QUALITY AT LOWER COST

During the last 50 years, every major industry except education has made enormous improvements in quality and productivity. Whereas other industries have made fundamental changes in core processes, the traditional education process – featuring a teacher lecturing to a class of students – has remained the norm. In fact, the static nature of the education industry actually yields *negative* annual productivity, as aggregate teacher salaries rise each year without commensurate increases in student learning.

The conventional wisdom states that the way to improve education is to reduce class size. However, research has demonstrated that reducing class size yields, at best, only modest benefits, with the most potential for improvement limited to the early elementary grades. In the middle school and high school years, learning does not improve until class size falls below 15 students. But since average class size is currently about 25, current costs would nearly double before any improvements would be realized, and, even then, experience teaches us that improvements would be minor. The fact remains that pupil/teacher ratios have declined significantly over several decades without comparable improvements in results.

If we redesign the system to take students out of "classes" and empower them as self-directed learners, while transforming teachers into facilitators, there is no limit to the quality that can be achieved at lower per-pupil costs.

A CLC for 150 multi-age learners could operate effectively with five facilitators at a cost of approximately $5,940 per-pupil, as shown below:

• Lead Facilitator	$ 90,000
• Experienced Facilitators (2)	110,000
• Inexperienced Facilitators (2)	80,000
• Payroll Taxes	30,000
• Benefits	70,000
• Building Depreciation	50,000
• Equipment Depreciation	90,000
• Interest Expense	165,000
• Cost of capital associated with land	55,000
• Maintenance, administration, supplies, etc.	151,000
Total ($5,940 per pupil in a CLC with 150 learners)	**$ 891,000**

This is a very conservative comparison that, if anything, over-states the comparative costs of the CLC approach, on several counts:

- Government and school district accounting principles do not provide for recording annual depreciation charges. Instead, capital items are reported in the year of acquisition or as debt payments are made. This can understate a school district's true cost in a given year. The provision for depreciation and interest expense in the CLC cost analysis should re-sult in a conservative comparison.

- Many schools are occupying land without cost. In order to make a conservative cost comparison, the CLC analysis as-sumes land acquisition costs for a CLC of $1 million and related interest expense of 5.5%.

- There are other weaknesses in government and school-dis-trict accounting that tend to understate the true costs re-ported by school districts. This, in turn, tends to widen the cost comparison between CLCs and traditional schools and, if corrected, would further increase the cost savings.

The estimated average per-pupil cost of $5,940 for a CLC, based on annualized costs for the 2002-03 school year, compares with the national average cost per-pupil in public schools of approximately $7,520 for the 2001-02 school year (latest available data). This indicates a cost savings of approximately 20%, which would translate into annual savings of about $75 billion. Since per-pupil costs vary widely by state, and even more by individual districts, the savings for many school districts could exceed 50%. Appendix D includes a summary of potential annual savings for each state.

Viewed narrowly, the annual 20% savings is achieved by the CLC model mainly by an increase in pupil/teacher ratio, from the national average of 17/1 to 30/1. However, the cost savings should be viewed not as a reduction of teaching re-sources, but as a more effective application of teacher and learner capabilities. The true difference is that a learner-cen-tered system continually assesses its alignment to purpose and its effectiveness and efficiency in meeting the needs of each learner, and thus continually improves its quality and produc-tivity.

These figures do not take into account the broad-based savings and economic benefits that would be realized from shortening the time needed to prepare students to enter the work force, as well as from higher productivity, reduced welfare, and reduction in the costs that stem from crime and related social problems.

The $75 billion savings is just the beginning. The system continues to develop, and there are no limits to the amount of savings and value created by the new education system.

A key component of the cost reduction available from the new model, which is not visible in the per-pupil cost comparisons, is relief from the ever-increasing burden of indebtedness that falls on students themselves. Today, going to college is considered essential; it is the ticket to higher-paying jobs. But increasingly, collegians are being loaded up with debt. Over time, however, as the new learning model takes hold and learner productivity increases, schooling beyond the ages of 18-20 will become unnecessary, except for those who opt for graduate school, and the baccalaureate degree will no longer be considered essential. Thus, parents and students will be spared the burdensome expense of college tuition, while lifetime earnings will also increase substantially. The net result, to the learners, will be greater short-term savings and enhanced long-term opportunity.

PART IV: GLIMPSING THE NEW MODEL'S FULL POTENTIAL

The ideas that have been discussed so far in this book reflect concepts that have been developed through the application of advanced theories of learning; tested in an actual CLC; and extrapolated, on a macro-basis, in order to present their overall societal benefit and impact. However, the tangible benefits of the new system can perhaps best be understood from the perspective of the individual learner.

To provide that perspective, this section, and the one that follows, attempt to portray what might happen in the daily lives of two learners and one facilitator at a CLC, at a time in the not-too-distant future when the CLCs' methods and approaches have become a normal and accepted part of the broader education system.

These stories illustrate the full range of experiences that can occur when the new system is fully in place – and the profound differences between these experiences and what is possible under the traditional system.

A Day in the Life of Two Learners

Kevin, age 17, and his sister Karen, age 13, would have been in the 11th and 7th grade, respectively, had they not left the traditional school system to join the new Community Learning Center, which follows principles of self-directed learning. The CLC has 150 multi-age learners, aged from 12 to 18. In addition, the CLC is currently considering modification of its admissions policies to include the ages from 6 to 11, and a pre-school program for 4 and 5-year-olds.

The CLC has a partnership with a nearby elementary school in which CLC learners serve as part-time teacher aides and role models, assisting in the teaching of traditional, basic skills of reading, writing, and arithmetic. They also assist in teaching the "new basics," including learning-to-learn skills and systems thinking. The CLC learners get a great deal of personal satisfaction from practicing the art of facilitation and other workplace skills, while helping others and fulfilling their community responsibilities.

Kevin enrolled five years ago, when the CLC opened. It was a difficult decision for him and his parents. They were concerned that the colleges of choice might not regard the CLC as highly as the traditional high school. On the other hand, Kevin felt that the freedom to take charge of his own learning would allow him to learn at a much higher level and to build a record of accomplishment that would allow him to distinguish himself to a far greater degree. This, he thought, is what would ultimately help him get into the college of his choice.

Kevin and his parents met with guidance counselors and visited a few college admissions officers. These meetings helped Kevin make his decision to become a "founding learner" of the CLC. In fact, it is a much easier decision for those who are now enrolling due to the CLC's well-documented successes, which includes high levels of learner and parental satisfaction with the CLC, high graduation rates, and a high level of acceptances of CLC graduates by the nation's top colleges and universities.

But even though Kevin found that the CLC met his needs, the decision regarding Karen's enrollment was not automatic. Her parents wanted to satisfy themselves that it would be appropriate to mix 13-year-old girls with young men, ages 16-to-18, even though Kevin would be around for at least the first few years.

Karen's parents met with the lead facilitator and learned that this matter had been carefully researched before the CLC was opened. In fact, no serious problems had been encountered at other multi-age, co-ed schools, as multi-age settings provide a more natural environment for young people to learn appropriate behavior and mutual respect.

The experience at the CLC confirmed this. Moreover, self-directed learning and democratic decision making at the CLC engendered self-reliance and personal responsibility, which had a very positive impact on interpersonal behaviors. Youngsters with freedom were much less likely to "act out" than were those subjected to rigid controls. Consequently, there had been no incidents that would pose any cause for concern.

Kevin was whistling as he arrived at the CLC at 7 a.m. – two hours "early" by conventional school time, but commonplace for CLC learners who simply love the place. This day Kevin had special reasons for an early start. Having served on the faculty of the adult high-tech program last evening, he had promised Ed, a high-level manager at a global manufacturing firm he was tutoring, that he would be available to help him make any necessary changes in the PowerPoint slide presentation they had worked on together. He sat down at one of the CLC's 75 PC workstations, half expecting to be called into action by Ed, or to receive the equivalent of a "high-five" thank-you for the work he had put into the presentation.

As Kevin booted-up and put his CLC-issued cell phone on "ready," he enjoyed a feeling of responsibility and openness to possibilities. After checking his e-mail, he made a note to call another new corporate contact, Sam, in order to arrange a follow-up meeting with one of the CLC's facilitators to explore Sam's company's interest in participating in the CLC internship program.

Since Kevin had to remain flexible pending this call, he decided this would be a good time to review the plans he had prepared for his 10:30 a.m. commitment to work in the nearby elementary school. Specifically, Kevin was working as a teacher's aide for a third grade class on "systems thinking." This would be the day for introducing the concept of "system archetypes," specifically the "limits-to-growth" archetype. He remembered how excited he was when he was first introduced to this concept and the "Aha!" feeling he experienced at realizing success would inevitably lead to failure if one did not anticipate the balancing factors. He recalled the notions of success leading to complacency and becoming a "victim of one's own success."

Kevin brushed up on notes he had taken during the CLC's seminar on systems thinking a few years ago. He then reviewed the notes from his own reading of *Urban Dynamics* by Jay W. Forrester, and *The Fifth Discipline*, by Peter Senge. After reviewing the notes, he decided not to start with a lecture. Instead, he decided it might be better to begin by leading a dialogue on the subject of situations that start well but lead to failure. That would lead to discovery of patterns of behavior and causal-loop diagramming of the underlying structure that portrays the limits-to-growth archetype. Kevin felt good about meeting his responsibilities in a creative way. The day had barely started and he already had a deep sense of accomplishment.

Kevin also used this time to refresh his thinking about his 9 a.m. commitment to participate in an on-line conference regarding a new cancer drug being developed by a global pharmaceutical company. He was amazed at the level of responsibility the company had given him, but perhaps, he thought, this was to be expected. They were constantly expressing how valuable he was to them because his questions had an objectivity that led to creative thinking.

Kevin was nearing the end of his six-month commitment to the project, but he wished he could continue through to the project's completion, since the new drug was in its final phase of testing. However, he recognized that others were in the queue for participating in the project. And, at any rate, he would soon be starting another internship, with a law firm, which would expose him to new opportunities closer to his personal aspirations.

At 8 a.m., Kevin's cell phone rang. It was Ed, calling to say he had reviewed the PowerPoint presentation and that with one minor change, he was very comfortable with it and would use it during an Internet conference later that day. Kevin took a minute to show him how to make the change. Ed thanked him profusely and offered Kevin a gratuity, which he turned down graciously, explaining that the fee paid to the CLC for the tutoring service was full payment for services rendered. "But would it be OK," asked Kevin, "if I added you to my list of references for college applications?" Ed said, "Sure thing." They made an appointment for their next tutorial session and briefly reviewed the topic and Ed's preparation requirements.

Kevin then participated in the drug company's conference call, which concluded precisely at 10 a.m. He really appreciated the respect they showed everyone by always wrapping up precisely on schedule, or even a few minutes early. It not only showed respect to the participants and made for effective teamwork; it also allowed full consideration of all agenda items, and enabled everyone to participate fully and stay to the call's completion. Kevin made a point to bring this issue up for discussion during the "CLC improvement" segment at the next CLC Board meeting.

Kevin arrived at the elementary school 10 minutes early. He reviewed his approach with the third grade teacher. She complimented Kevin and told him that she would be present during the first 10 minutes, and again for 10 minutes at the end. Meanwhile, in case he needed her, she said, she would be meeting with some parents in a nearby conference room.

When she returned shortly before lunchtime, she was delighted to see about twenty flip-chart sheets taped to the wall, representing the work of ten teams, each made up of three learners. The last team was in the midst of making its presentation on examples of the "limits-to-growth" archetype. Kevin had a few of the learners assisting him as co-facilitators. The class was responding with energy and interest. They were actively involved. Their thoughts counted and were useful. The teacher thanked Kevin with a warm smile, which he returned, offering a series of self-study ideas for her to recommend to her students. He said he would be back next week to lead a dialogue about the "success-to-the-successful" archetype. As Kevin left, the learners rose and gave him a rousing "hip, hip, hooray!" He sighed deeply, proud and grateful for the opportunity to serve them.

Later, over a lunch cooked by the CLC learner-chefs of the month, Kevin was enjoying bantering with his friends when one of the facilitators came by and asked him to see her later in the day when he had a moment. After lunch, and a brief game of touch football, he met up with her in the Great Room.

The facilitator told Kevin that his name was among those picked at random for service on the Judicial Committee for next September. He checked his schedule and said that he would modify his plans accordingly. He agreed to re-read the CLC Constitution and Judicial Committee operating procedures, and to attend a few of the committee meetings before serving his term.

There was a presumption that learners would remain in the CLC at least until their 18th birthday. Kevin, at age 17, had already demonstrated mastery of the competencies set forth in the "Graduate Profile," as required for certification by the CLC Assembly of learners, parents and community members. He decided to graduate after his 18th birthday in June, so that in the meantime, he could participate in a few more internships that would expose him to a wider range of career possibilities.

Also, he was interested in a work-study program that some of the prestigious law firms had developed as an alternative to the traditional college track. CLC graduates could join the firm upon graduation and continue their formal education for three months a year, for up to five years, at leading universities throughout the world. Competition for the best candidates was resulting in tactics similar to those used by professional basketball teams seeking to recruit high school graduates. This approach would save Kevin's family over $100,000 in tuition and related expenses at a top-tier university, while generating an additional four years of earnings. He had talked this over with the facilitators, and they had agreed to fully back his plans.

Kevin understood that his plans for personal development and his quest to become a lawyer would require a much broader education than the mere study of law itself. This would be particularly true if he sought to specialize in environmental regulation, in which he had a passionate interest. So Kevin, with the help of facilitators schooled in biology, physics, and general systems theory, designed a program to maximize his learning in these areas, while also reinforcing his strong foundation in technical writing and effective presentations. Today, at 5 p.m., Kevin had a two-hour appointment with three of these facilitators to review his personal learning program for the remaining year at the CLC. Instead of the "goof-off" senior year many students would experience in a traditional high school, Kevin would be applying his learning skills at his highest level ever and would earn a sum equivalent to the cost of his entire college education. Kevin's commitment to the CLC would be strengthened, and he would continue to involve himself deeply in the life of the CLC, helping others to learn and to find their own pathways to success.

Kevin had a few hours before his scheduled meeting with the facilitators. He spent the extra time in a one-hour dialogue with others on the front-page news story of the day – and then got involved in a game of tennis doubles.

As a result of this recreational activity, Kevin felt refreshed for his 5 p.m. meeting. He was glad he had set up the meeting for the end of the regular school day, as it did not wrap up until after 7 p.m. During the meeting, Kevin got a great deal of feedback on his plans. He would reflect on the suggestions, and, after a review with peers, mentors, internship advisors, and his parents, he would file an amended plan with the facilitators.

Kevin walked home with a sense of exhilaration and gave his parents and sister a briefing, over dinner, on the highlights of his momentous decision: to pursue an internship with a major law firm that would yield direct entry into the legal profession, with a specialization in environmental regulation.

After dinner, Kevin was off to rehearse for his role in Shakespeare's *Hamlet*, the current month's CLC play, undertaken in conjunction with the other CLCs in town. He laughed to himself: How had he, of all people, come to be selected to play the role of indecisive Prince Hamlet? He thought to himself, "I think I'll reinterpret *Hamlet* tonight!"

Karen, at 13, was at a very different stage in her life than her brother Kevin. She benefited greatly from the opportunity to see him develop as a co-member of the CLC "learning community." If it not been for the CLC multi-age concept, she would never have observed him in action as a learner and as a leader. He was a source of inspiration for her. A wonderful, mutually supportive relationship was developing between them.

Even though Kevin was almost five years older than Karen, he learned a great deal from her. She was a free spirit, keeping all of life's options open. He often balanced his own thought processes by asking himself, "How would Karen address this?" He felt blessed, knowing that he had Karen as a friend for life.

Thank goodness, they had found the CLC! Had they both continued in traditional schools, they probably would have ended up like most siblings, robbed of common experiences, barely interacting with each other, and actually competing with each other for the highest test scores and grades. How different it was to be part of a learning community, free to develop at their own pace and in their own way, while sharing a common purpose of enhancing the community.

Karen has a passionate commitment to the CLC. In her first year in the CLC, Karen noted there were no learning-disabled or "special-ed" kids enrolled at the CLC, and made recruiting such students into a personal cause. She raised the issue at the CLC's Town Meeting and Assembly, and led the effort to amend the CLC charter to seek representation by special-ed learners in the same proportion as they were registered in the town's public schools. The result: five such learners were now enrolled at the CLC.

It turned out that three of the so-called "learning disabled" students were not learning disabled at all. The regular school administration had misinterpreted their behavior, and had assigned them to separate special-ed classes. In fact, they simply learned in a different way than what was considered the norm. Frustrated by the restrictions and rigidity of the traditional system, they became disruptive under the traditional classroom structure.

But these learners flourished in the CLC's self-directed learning environment. Without a teacher lecturing in front of the classroom, requiring silence and constant attention, there was reduced possibility for disruption. Also, self-directed learning enabled the special-ed learners to exercise their creativity, which enabled them to make a valuable contribution to the CLC.

The two learners who did prove to be truly learning-disabled, one of them autistic, also served to enhance the learning community. Many of the other learners loved caring for them. Everyone learned one of life's most important truths: personal meaning is derived from helping others.

Karen felt good about having led this important change in the CLC. In her very first year, at the age of 13, she had made an important contribution to her community – and thus completed a rite of passage to adulthood. Instead of just singing songs about self-esteem, she had a genuine sense of accomplishment.

After Karen had opened the doors of the CLC to the so-called learning-disabled, she had begun serving as a teacher's aide in the special-ed classes of the traditional school system. The school administrators were wary of Karen's involvements in their special-ed classes, expecting to see an article in the local paper about the railroading of so many students into special-ed categories. However, through having taken CLC seminars on systems thinking and conflict resolution, Karen recognized that the solution did not lie in rebelling against the school administration, which could retaliate against the CLC. Instead, she saw that the best way would be in working with the traditional school leadership to enhance public awareness of the need for fundamental change in the system and in building more CLCs. Beyond learning subject matter, Karen had acquired practical wisdom and a sense of how to make change happen – even in traditional institutions.

Now, Karen is spending a good deal of time studying the causes and medical treatments for learning disabilities in children. In just one year's time, she has acquired as much knowledge about learning disabilities as the typical college graduate majoring in this area would acquire in four years. She is currently seeking enrollment in on-line graduate studies that will provide her with the equivalent of a doctorate in learning disabilities. She intends to complete this program before she graduates from the CLC.

Karen also has a passion for modern dance. By pushing away several of the computer stations, all of which are on wheels, a stage is created – and Karen can often be seen dancing in this cleared performance space. Karen plays music suitable to the mood of the day and begins her dance, beckoning others to join her as she goes. Most everyone watches with awe, and some who never imagined themselves as dancers join in uninhibitedly. No one knows exactly what the meaning of the dance is, but they all are entranced by the exercise of pure freedom. After fifteen minutes or so, the dancing ends and feeling refreshed, everyone returns to their conversations, play and work.

The facilitators have observed the dance scene, impressed with Karen's display of freedom, self-expression and gracefulness. With deep admiration, they feel themselves being influenced by her and learning from her.

A Day in the Life of a Facilitator

Linda, a veteran teacher in a traditional school, joined the CLC team of five facilitators last year, four years after the CLC opened. After only one year, she regarded the CLC, with its 150 learners, aged 12 to 18, as her extended family.

For over twenty years she had gone to work every day with a sense of foreboding. She knew that several times during each school day she would have to ignore students who needed individual attention, because taking the time would jeopardize her ability to fully cover the lesson plan for that day. She had long ago made her compromise with the system, and in fact, the principal and superintendent had complimented her on her ability to "control" her classroom. However, her guilt actually increased, and her initial feeling of total commitment to her students eroded over the years.

But now, all that has changed. She starts work at the CLC every day truly excited about her newfound empowerment and about the plans and possibilities in store for her. She looks forward to working with learners and with other members of the community to facilitate individual learning and to make the CLC a better and more resourceful place for them.

On this day, Linda arrived at the CLC at 8:15 a.m. About half of the learners were already there, engaged in conversation, work, study, and play. She strolled through the CLC, smiling hello to all those looking her way, and responding to the banter directed at her. She stopped at the bulletin board to see if any of the learners had petitioned for a special seminar or dialogue. She noted the schedule of "learning-to-learn" seminars for that day and the learners who would lead them – along with a designated facilitator for seminars whose leaders needed additional support. She checked the CLC's Web-based digest of leading news sources, checking to see whether there was a likelihood of a request for a dialogue on a news item of the day.

Linda spent a half-hour at her workstation responding to e-mails from learners, parents, facilitators, and internship managers. At 8:50 a.m., she walked into the conference room for a 10-minute conference with the other facilitators. Nancy, the facilitator team-leader, used her computer to project each facilitator's schedule for the day onto the white-board. Everyone input their changes, and the final schedule was downloaded to their hand held computers. The team was reminded that the two-hour guided tour of the CLC by a delegation of educators from The Netherlands, including that country's education minister, would be handled by two learners. Nancy invited the facilitators to join the group in the conference room for a portion of the 30-minute wrap-up, assuming that at least one facilitator would cover the Great Room.

Linda headed for the 9:00 a.m. meeting of the Judicial Committee (JC). The JC, composed of five learners and a non-voting facilitator-advisor, is provided for in the CLC Constitution; it operates like a court to protect learners' rights and to foster cooperation and order. Learners who believe that their rights or CLC rules have been violated can bring charges against the offending learner and seek appropriate constraints and penalties.

Linda had initially been skeptical that this approach could work, and was wary of operating without the absolute authority she had wielded as a teacher in the traditional school. However, she was soon convinced of the wisdom of this approach, not only as a tool for maintaining order, but also as a way for learners to understand and practice the responsibilities of citizenship. Linda, as the faculty-advisor to the Judicial Committee for this month, would observe the process and be available for questions about due process and sentencing issues. Today's docket consisted of just two minor cases. The defendants pleaded guilty, as they did in over 90% of all cases, and were appropriately sentenced. The learners wrote up the cases and transmitted the paperwork to the President of the School Meeting for inclusion into the official record at the next School Meeting. With the JC meeting ending sooner than normal, Linda decided to spend time interfacing with learners in the Great Room.

Linda strolled through the large open Great Room of the CLC. She loved the sound of the place. It told her that freedom was being exercised. Instead of the silence of a traditional classroom, there was the soft buzz of life, punctuated with laughter and occasional shrieks from joyful learning, discovery, and kidding around. The sound was a mixture of the murmur of a beehive with the excited chatter of a restaurant filled to capacity, only softer, out of unconscious consideration for others. It was a new sound: the noise of self-organizing youth. It was created by dozens of groups of self-directed learners – engaged in a wide variety of learning activities in the form of conversation, play and purposeful work.

When she was new to the CLC, Linda had felt that she should initiate interaction with the learners; in fact, she had felt a need to do so. She would ask learners what they were working on, briefly review the work in process, and offer unsolicited advice. While this was far more effective than her role as lecturer in the traditional classroom, it did not take long before she learned that the far more effective approach was to simply respond to learners' questions. And rather than supply answers (which she rarely had anyway), she would respond with questions that would help them to discover the barriers they were confronting. Often she would refer them to other learners whom she knew had grappled with similar issues. Linda had come to view herself as a teacher by example, a model learner and a model leader.

Linda also enjoyed the opportunity to interact with and learn from her peers. When she had been a teacher in the traditional classroom, she liked being the sole authority and the "sage on the stage." But having been in such an isolated environment, she now realizes how much she had missed. Her new sense of empowerment has been exhilarating. Beyond the benefits of personal and professional development, collaborating with four other facilitators in the CLC allowed her to work with professionals and learners in the co-design and co- management of a much richer learning environment. In addition to working with individual learners, she loves the challenge of connecting with the community, arranging internships, mentorships and special programs for the CLC.

At 10 a.m., Linda led a seminar on Systems Thinking. The fifteen learners who signed up had already studied and done the pre-reading, along with several exercises on the Internet. The group was motivated by the desire to serve as facilitators for the 3rd grade elementary school class on Systems Thinking, and to eventually qualify for some of the internship programs for which Systems Thinking and computer modeling were a prerequisite. Linda used Shakespeare's *Hamlet* as a source for applying the principles of causal loop diagramming. She relished the challenge of exposing learners to the classics as a by-product of their acquiring learning-to-learn skills.

Linda had a "business lunch" with Don, the Director of Training for a large manufacturing firm located nearby. Don had read of the great results being achieved at the CLC and wanted to learn more. He was a key member of a reengineering project at his firm, which was redesigning work methods to achieve "just-in-time" manufacturing. One aspect of this change entailed shifting away from periodic conduct of formal training classes to self-directed, on-line tutorials, accessed by the learner on the job, as needed. The outcome of the meeting was a decision to explore an "exchange program" in which Linda would serve as a paid summer intern at the firm, participating on the firm's reengineering team, and for Don and two of his staff, working with a group of learners, to study the CLC to identify areas of potential improvement. This would in all likelihood lead to a formal internship program.

Linda returned to the CLC at 2 p.m., in time to serve as an observer-advisor for a learner-led seminar on "effective presentations," one of a series of seminars on learning-to-learn skills. Last year, Linda had taken a three-day course on effective presentations with a world-class training firm. After practicing the art of presenting, and leading dozens of seminars at the CLC, she had conducted a series of "Train the Trainer" courses for CLC learners interested in enhancing their presentation skills and serving as facilitators themselves. Juanita, the learner-facilitator for that day, had progressed from being a poor performer to one of the best presenters, and was now "certified" to serve as facilitator for this skill at the CLC. At the end of the two-hour seminar, Linda led a dialogue among the participating learners that provided feedback to Juanita on her performance. As a result, the learners were learning the art of facilitation, as well as the art of effective presentations.

Linda played an hour of tennis with three of the learners before going on to a 5 to 7 p.m. meeting with facilitators and Kevin (the student we've already met) regarding his personal learning plans. Linda did not mind working late whenever that made sense for the learners. Unlike traditional schools, there was no homework and no tests to grade. But learning was always going on after school hours – and a good deal of it took place at the CLC. In fact, many of the learners had volunteered to serve on the faculty for the adult learning program, which included courses in technology, learning-to-learn and creative thinking, among others.

As Linda left the CLC at 7 p.m. that evening, she reflected on her day. She had a wonderful sense of accomplishment, on several levels. She had practiced her art to her personal-best standards. She had expanded the reach of the CLC. She had been creative in exposing learners to new horizons. And her relationships with learners and peers were deepening.

She asked herself: "Did I respond to every child in need?" Reflecting on that question, she had a new insight: the problems that had gone unattended in the traditional system were largely caused by the system itself, not by any lack of attention by her. For more than 20 years, she had felt guilty for not doing what she had set out to do as a new teacher. But in reality, despite her best efforts, and for a variety of reasons beyond her control, a great many students in the traditional system were simply set up to fail on day-one. Linda decided that she would work with her colleagues in traditional schools to replicate CLCs and transform the education system.

PART V: SELECTED PUBLIC POLICY ISSUES

Special Education: The System Is Disabled

The stories told above illustrate a number of key benefits of the learner-centered education system. One of the most dramatic opportunities takes place in the sphere of special education. One of the clearest indications that the education system is not student-centered, is essentially inflexible and is highly irrelevant to crucial needs lies in the segregation and so-called "special" treatment that is afforded to students labeled as "learning disabled."

In every community, disabled people strive to fit in to the maximum extent possible. We admire such people, and our humanity is strengthened by our individual and collective efforts to assist the disabled among us. However, in our traditional education system, those who are learning-disabled, as defined by bureaucratic school officials, are taken out of the mainstream of students and placed in classes composed of other special-ed students.

How can this segregation be consistent with the goal of living as normal a life as possible – let alone the precept of equal opportunity for all?

At first glance, the motivation for affording this segregated treatment may appear to be thoughtful and benevolent. It may seem to be in the best interests of the child and may be in accordance with parental wishes. However, it constitutes far from ideal treatment.

Is it possible that the rationale for segregating such students is that they are not compatible with the machine-like, assembly-line structure of the traditional school system – hampering its efficiency as a production tool? Or is it that the disabled child might be disruptive in a traditional classroom, which is kept as quiet as a morgue, while the teacher recites a lesson and leads the class in a contrived question and answer session?

It gets worse. Is the special-ed classification also motivated in part by desire to generate more financial aid? Is the special-ed classification also motivated in part by a desire to report higher test scores, since such students historically have been excluded from the measurement process?

The following story, based on a situation observed by the author, may not be an isolated event.

At a community focus meeting in an urban area, in 1994, convened to evaluate opportunities for improvement in the public schools, the moderator asked attendees: are there any comments or concerns you have about the school system?

An immigrant Hispanic mother took the floor. Trembling with a mixture of rage and fear, she declared softly, in a heavily accented voice: "They're using my child." She said, "A school official gave me a release form to sign, within twenty minutes, to concur to a transfer into special-ed – or else my child will be put into a mental institution. They're using my child for budget reasons...forcing me to allow them to take my child out of the regular track."

This tragedy should never occur when learning-disabled students seek to enroll in the public schools. It can essentially be prevented by the new education system. The CLCs would admit these children proportionately to their numbers in the local community. They would find themselves to be warmly received and cared for by the other learners. In cases of only mild disability, the students will lose any distinctive symptoms as they blend into the self-directed life of the center. With no authoritative figure at the head of a classroom, demanding silence and so-called "good behavior," they will not have to make a Herculean effort to sit still. There is simply no way to disrupt the learning that goes on in a CLC.

Such treatment should not be regarded as a special accommodation to the special-ed learners. Mainstreaming, or "inclusion," should be regarded as a constitutional right of special-ed learners. The situation simply represents the real world and the toleration that is ethically required of all who desire to treat such people as fellow human beings.

All of the learners in a CLC quickly come to understand that such children have rights, and that caring for the weak or infirm is a civic responsibility for all of us. If parents of special-ed students wish to continue the segregated arrangement for their children, they should be accommodated. Yet society's greater good is served by such children's accommodation in the schools established for all of us. The CLCs, because they are focused on the needs of each student, provide the best way of addressing these special needs without disrupting an imaginary "common" pace or flow – which in any event is an illusory construct.

Once a significant number of CLCs are functioning, there will be sufficient evidence to demonstrate that a high proportion of the learning-disabled are not disabled at all – and that instead, it is the traditional education system that is disabled.

The Compelling Case for the New Education System in Impoverished Urban Areas

Despite federal, state, and local efforts to provide good schools and quality programs, poor urban areas have been mired for decades in an educational crisis. This situation is exacerbated by the growing Digital Divide. Relatively few children in the nation's inner cities will graduate from high school prepared for jobs as "knowledge workers" in the Information Age.

These children are among those with the greatest need for the benefits of educational reform. Our nation's commitment to equal opportunity dictates that we spare no effort to bring them into the new education system as soon as possible. Indeed, the certainty of their success with the new learning model will do much to catalyze interest by suburban communities who, themselves, are too complacent about their own need to change.

Many observers might be skeptical about the readiness of inner-city youth for the less structured schooling process represented by CLCs, along with the personal responsibility such institutions entail. One might reasonably expect concerns about chaos and uncontrollable situations. However, this is merely a variation of what President George W. Bush has called the "soft bigotry of low expectations." In an empowering and non-hierarchical setting, all children respond positively – none more so than a disadvantaged child – to being treated with respect and as an equal to adults.

Can a child in the inner city learn? They learn very well. Indeed, they are streetwise. Yet too often, their schooling is the product of misguided educational theories – well-intended, yet detrimental in their ultimate impact. If traditional school systems pose disciplinary challenges for the middle-class student, then imagine how structured and controlling the system must feel to a child whose images of authority figures may derive

primarily from law enforcement officials.   The traditional
school system, widely blamed for its high failure rate in the inner city, is no different there than in the middle-class suburbs.
Instead, it does not work for inner-city children for the same
reasons it does not work anywhere – precisely because it is too
structured and too controlling. The new learning model, with its
self-directed, self-paced approach, offers new hope for such
children. It does not treat them as different, disadvantaged or
disturbed.   Instead, it minimizes their differences, promotes a
healthy self-assessment, and enables them to design a unique
pathway to success, with assistance from their peers and facilitators.

Other features of the new learning model that are ex-
tremely important for inner-city youth are access to the most
advanced technology and the presence of multiple facilitators
who remain with the same cohort of learners for a number of
years and thus get to know each other very well. The apprenticeship and internship features that we have covered in detail
are also crucial. They result in true mentoring relationships with
successful adults, on the job – not merely once-a-month lunch
with a volunteer – that can help bridge the great chasm between
the inner city and the downtown business district and cultural
center. That gap is much harder to overcome than the differences in test scores.

The location of small CLCs that are situated within a
short walk from home, and that are open in the evenings to provide adult learning programs, will also allow evening access by
community youth to computers and other resources. This will
go a long way to eliminate the Digital Divide – the relative lack
of access to computers and other communication technologies
that threatens to widen the gap between the haves and the have-
nots.

The issue of neighborhood safety, so real in the inner
cities, is ameliorated by small CLCs located near home. Today,
students may have to walk through a number of gang territories
in order to get to school. Many decide to join gangs in order to
gain a measure of defense against gang attack; this, of course,
only makes the gang problem worse. CLCs in the neighborhood
would largely eliminate this problem.

Also, children in the inner city who want to get an education are often taunted as "wannabe's" and subject to abuse

and physical harm. The neighborhood CLC will be viewed as an important community resource, and enable local children to feel much more secure in their own neighborhood.

There is also the issue of cost. As mentioned elsewhere, the new education system will cost considerably less than the traditional system: $5,940 per student for the new system, versus $7,520 for the traditional system. The per-pupil cost for inner-city schools should be comparable to the cost in other schools.

A number of cities are disputing state funding formulas that allocate more funds per-pupil to suburban schools. They want the states to "level-up" their funding to equalize the situation. They should, instead, implement the new system, and then demand that the state "level down," which would save the states and cities a great deal of money, while making resources available for other purposes, including re-development of the cities. While such leveling-down may seem counterintuitive, the situation will only get worse unless city leaders take this bold and necessary initiative.

There are a number of other issues that present challenges to bringing relevance to education in the inner-city, such as crime, drugs, teenage pregnancy, and other social issues. However, much progress on these issues can be made simply by substituting a learner-centered system that addresses the needs of each individual student. Indeed, the community links that are a crucial component of CLCs will make them especially relevant to addressing seemingly recalcitrant community problems. To reinterpret an African proverb for modern times: "It takes free, creative children to continually remake a community."

Parental Choice, Vouchers, and Privatization

It would be naïve to propose a new theory of education without addressing the very serious governmental issues that could impede its realization. A new theory of schooling, the prospect of significant cost savings, and well-intentioned teachers are not sufficient to effect fundamental change in the public school system. Intransigent government bureaucracy, and other forces of resistance, must be countered, and political power must shift in favor of the users of education services.

On a policy level, this change begins with parental choice. In view of compulsory education laws and the monopoly power of public schools, parents should be granted the ability to select the schools their children will attend. This will make all schools more responsive to parents and learners, and create a more competitive environment for purposes of enhancing efficiency.

Still, mere choice is not enough to achieve fundamental change. Parents should not be subject to the "tyranny of the majority." If a sufficient number of parents subscribe to a different theory of schooling than that of the traditional authoritative model, and wish to send their children to a school that is based on the principles of self-directed learning, the school district should react in a responsive manner and establish a CLC.

Many states have passed charter school laws that enable teachers, parents, and community members to establish "alternative schools." This approach could be followed if the district fails to be responsive, or if the founders of such a school desire the additional financial and operating independence afforded by a charter.

The simple structure of CLCs means that a great number of these facilities can be built inexpensively and that practically speaking, parents will therefore have more choices regarding where to send their children than have been available under the traditional school model.

For many years, a number of economists, public policy experts, and business executives have recommended vouchers as a means of maximizing parental choice in education and forcing schools to compete in a more responsive and efficient manner. Under this approach, parents are given vouchers to defray the cost of non-public education services purchased from an approved institution, whether these schools are for-profit or not-for-profit.

However, vouchers have not won majority support among parents. Perhaps a key reason is that parents situated in suburban communities that have "good" schools, at least as the public perceives them, wish to remain insulated from encroachment by children from impoverished areas. Until now, the only voucher plans implemented have been in inner-city communities, where parents have opted to send their children to religious schools.

Surprisingly, the debate over vouchers has not included the suggestion that public funding of education should be abolished, although this would require the states to amend their constitutions, which currently require a "free" public education. But a tuition-based system would provide an incentive for parents to demand that schools perform to the maximum and that students complete their formal schooling in the shortest possible time.

Under a tuition-based system, cost savings would be passed on to consumers due to the efficiencies demanded by those attuned to such issues. A tuition-funded, fee-based system would put pressure on secondary schools to arrange apprenticeship and internship programs to enhance the quality of learning, and private companies might be much more adept at meeting this need than government-run schools.

Some unexpected players might get involved. Many of the nation's more than 3,000 private four-year colleges and nearly 1,100 community colleges are already utilizing a tuition-funded and fee-based system and might expand their reach to include K-12. Such initiatives would result in a holistic education system, leveraging the best teaching resources and compressing the time for formal schooling – perhaps via a K-14 or even more aggressive program. By contrast, under a government-financed system, costs tend to increase, as there is little incentive to cut costs.

It would appear that a system of publicly financed "free" schools would have greater opportunities to practice grass-roots democracy and community improvement than private schools. However, there is no reason why private schools, whether non-profit or for-profit, could not be governed as a "pure" democracy, as is called for in our vision of a new education system.

A number of school districts have outsourced to contractors the operation of all or some of their schools through multi-year contracts. However, for the most part, these outsourcings represent attempts to operate more efficiently and improve the traditional teaching model, rather than to fundamentally transform the education system.

Edison Schools, Inc., by far the largest of these contractors, with operations in over 20 states, serving approximately 110,000 students during the 2002 school year, has a business model that relies on achieving administrative cost savings generated by increasing its scale of operations. The company has made gains in student test scores, but after several years of operations, through 2002, Edison has yet to make a profit.

Education companies should persuade school districts to adopt the new education system described in this book, based on self-directed learning and multi-age groupings. Using this model, the opportunities for cost savings are so great that the school districts now inclined to outsource their school operations would be well advised to initiate a prototype Community Learning Center program and base the pricing of their outsourcing contracts on replication of the new model. Doing this would allow them to retain most of the cost savings.

For-profit education companies are well established in many countries. In contrast to public schools and private non-profit schools, for-profit education companies have a need to grow both revenues and profits. In fact, we are witnessing the emergence of transnational, for-profit education companies at the elementary, secondary, and higher education levels. And child-care companies, increasingly becoming pervasive, will expand vertically to include early elementary grades.

As for-profit education companies grow, they will see no reason to hand over their customers to higher education. The K-12 companies that adopt the vision of self-directed learning will be able to improve productivity sufficiently enough to accomplish college-level goals at very low cost, as greater numbers of older students mean that more learners would be available to serve as teacher-aides.

Similarly, for-profit colleges will expand to the K-12 market. For now, they are competing for the adult and lifelong learning market, employing distance learning and regular courses.

Because so many governments are pouring more money into an obsolete system, costs keep accumulating without results. This excess funding creates an increasingly attractive market for education companies. At this time of great change and great opportunity for both public and private educators, bold action is required. Educators should not reengineer or tinker with the existing system. Instead, they should understand the emergent forces at work in education and fundamentally transform the system.

As the wave of change forms on the horizon, educators should not wait until it breaks and thus risk being swept away. They should paddle out to meet it as it forms, and surf it all the way to shore.

Educating the Nation: A Responsibility of the States

The founding fathers believed strongly that a well-educated public was vitally important for a well-functioning democracy and the preservation of liberty. However, they made no provision in the U.S. Constitution for any federal role in education. It was not even an issue of debate. As expressly provided in the Constitution, any powers not specifically ceded to the federal government were reserved for the states. And in accordance with this prerogative, each of the states has provided in its constitution for a child's right to a public education.

The United States, except for a handful of mainly Commonwealth nations, is the only country in the world that does not have a national ministry responsible for regulating and running the nation's education system, and even those exceptions are far more controlling of education at the national level than is the U.S. Some elements of national control are the application of a national curriculum and national exams, which have not been features of the American system. While a number of other countries are beginning to empower local governments and educators, and loosening regulations over schools in order to make them more innovative, mirroring changes in organizational theory taking hold in the private sector, the United States appears to be moving in the opposite direction by increasing the federal role in elementary and secondary education.

During the last 20 years, education has moved to the top of the domestic political agenda. The context of the national and local debate has been: (a) concern over the lagging performance of inner-city minorities; (b) the linkage of school performance to global economic competitiveness; (c) school safety; (d) teacher quality and accountability; (e) equality of access to schools and colleges; and (f) parental choice, and related issues of vouchers and outsourcing. There are other issues, including how to teach reading (phonics vs. whole language), the importance of math and science, technology and the Internet, inclusion of special-ed students, and English as a second language.

Despite the magnitude of the changes wrought by the Information Age and the increased importance attached to education in this new era, the ideas and programs offered by political leaders have not included anything fundamentally different or new. These initiatives continue to buttress the traditional system of education.

President George W. Bush, who took office in January 2001, promptly proposed legislation to "leave no child behind." This legislation was subsequently enacted by the Congress and signed by Bush in January 2002. The law puts heavy emphasis on annual tests for students in third-through-eighth grades, which many believe will put the nation on the road to a national curriculum. With the resulting emphasis in schools on preparation for the exams, test scores will probably rise enough to enable officials to declare the program a success. However, this "fix" of the system will come at a cost: failure to make the fundamental changes the system requires. Increasing the federal government's role in education will limit innovation and move away from the practice of democracy at a grass-roots level.

The political solution to the many issues facing America's education system lies in leaving the administration of education to the states, their localities, and individual citizen initiatives. These make up countless laboratories within which successful educational principles can be discovered, tested and replicated on a broader scale.

Reserving the fix to state or local players will also help to cope with an even more serious challenge to democracy and representative government that is emerging, due to the accelerating pace of change. Local players are best suited to develop the solutions that are most appropriate to their children's needs. Keeping the administration of education at the state and local level provides a rich field of practice for grass roots democracy and sound democratic decision making.

This does not mean that the federal government should do nothing with regard to education. Besides the "bully pulpit," it could conduct research, subsidize innovation at a local level, and implement new learning models in schools under its jurisdiction, including those located in Washington, D.C. and at military bases.

PART VI: MAKING THE TRANSITION

Each school district's leadership should engage the administration, teachers, and community in a visioning process that creates powerful support for change and a commitment to create a number of CLCs. The establishment of multiple CLCs in a given community would strengthen pioneering facilitators, enhance prospects for success, broaden community support, and increase the pool of learning resources needed for the roll-out phase. The visioning process should also result in a moratorium on construction of large, obsolete, factory-like schools.

Savings from the new education model will be sufficient to recoup the cost of reconfiguring school facilities and adding enhanced technology. Nonetheless, there will be an initial need for capital outlays. If capital funds from the district or state are not forthcoming or are insufficient to meet the modest expenditures required for the prototype program, leasing or operating funds could be used. Grant funds may also be available or pursued for the program.

While the prospects for cost savings may be a driving force among some stakeholders in lobbying for educational change, the paramount focus should be on the total transformation of the system. The prospect of reduced funding due to cost reductions should not pose a source of resistance to change by teachers and union leaders, as improvements in quality and productivity will justify salary increases for deserving teachers. And there should be no fear of teacher layoffs, since the transition will take place over a period of five-to-fifteen years, during which time substantial natural attrition in the teacher ranks will occur.

If district leaders do not undertake fundamental change, groups of parents, teachers, and concerned citizens should apply for state funds to create charter schools.

The greatest barrier to change is complacency on the part of parents who feel that their children's schools are performing adequately, and who do not understand that a fundamentally different model of education is needed. Their complacency calls to mind the fable of the boiled frog. In that fable, one frog slowly simmered to death in a pot of water under a low flame, while another placed into boiling water immediately jumped out. As with the simmered frog, there appears to be no visible crisis to galvanize the public into action.

The public will not be moved to demand a different education system through dire predictions alone. However, the public will respond to a clear vision of a better future for their children, especially if they can visit a prototype CLC in order to see the new education system in action.

At a prototype CLC, visitors are not likely to see a fully integrated kindergarten through high school (K-12). While this prototype CLC will eventually serve children of all ages, it typically begins operating with children in the 12-to-18 or 12-to-16 age groups, i.e., the students who are in middle school and high school. This step "seeds" the CLC with mature learners who serve as a resource for the younger learners entering in succeeding years. This approach assures that current students get exposure to the new learning concepts. Alternatively, some prototype CLCs grow into the K-12 environment by starting out with a cohort of 6-12 year-olds (K-6th graders), who benefit immediately from the principles of self-directed learning. This defers start-up of pre-kindergarten programs and adult after-school programs until the CLC has passed through its start-up phase.

The process of fully transitioning to a CLC-based system will need to overcome the conventional wisdom as it relates to assessment and accountability in the schools. Specifically, it will have to deal with public policy in one key area: testing. The federal government and many states have recently enacted legislation that puts emphasis on standardized tests, whereas the vision for a new education system espoused here would eliminate traditional testing in favor of the much more robust methods of assessment and accountability previously mentioned.

In the new education system, self-directed learners will not ignore federal and state mandates with regard to testing. They know they must be able to test well in order to gain entry into colleges of their choice and, thus, gain employment after graduation. Being highly self-motivated, they will do what is necessary to achieve their objectives. In fact, because learners play a key role in the process of designing what goes on at the CLC and because the reputation of the CLC is important to them, they will devise programs to ensure that they will achieve their life goals.

To avoid the appearance of ducking accountability, and to demonstrate the effectiveness of the new learning model, CLC learners will take the standardized tests required of all students in the school district. And as the CLCs demonstrate their superiority, learners will lead in making the case for transforming the traditional education system and ending the newly mandated, but obsolete methods of testing.

PART VII: CALL TO ACTION

In the Information Age, learning has become the new frontier. In every industrialized nation, and in many developing nations, improving education is a top priority. New methods of learning are being explored by ministries of education, public and private schools, and education companies throughout the world.

America's position of world leadership has been a product of its commitment to democratic principles, free markets, and social cohesion. This has made America the "land of opportunity." To facilitate equal opportunity, America has made access to education an individual right and a practical reality.

America's future depends on how well it meets the challenge of reinventing education to anticipate the needs of the new era in which change is a constant. We must design a system of education that continually restructures itself, that provides everyone an equal opportunity to reach their potential, and that equips the body politic for democratic decision making in a more complex world. Bringing the new education system into existence, and facilitating its continuous redesign in accordance with current and future customer needs will require the participation of each major sector of society.

Federal Actions

As explained elsewhere in this book, the federal government should leave the primary role of education to the states, but should also retain and build on its role in promoting research and development in education and the schooling process. The need to transform education is a national imperative. However, recent federal legislation puts the emphasis on increasing standardized testing, which reinforces the traditional education system.

It is likely that the recent federal legislation will result in improved test scores, but less love of learning and less relevant learning. The increased emphasis on testing, based on principles of extrinsic motivation and competition among students, will favor those who are succeeding in the traditional system. Many poorly performing students will drop out, creating the illusion of improvements in test scores. The resulting gap between adequately performing and poorly performing students is likely to widen, and the learning process will increase its bias toward mediocrity.

Increased emphasis on testing represents "more of the same." It reinforces the obsolete model of education at a time when greater incentives to innovate are needed.

President Bush should declare war on mediocrity in America's education system and schooling process. Instead of prescribing tests and micromanaging the details of education processes, the federal government should encourage new models of education, such as self-directed learning in multi-age settings. The slogan, "leave no child behind" should be subordinate to "aspire to your full potential." To guarantee this, a Child Bill of Rights should be introduced as a constitutional amendment.

The president should articulate a vision for a new education system that would capture the imagination of the American people and provoke innovative action at the state and local level. A presidential vision should detail the federal role as catalyst for fundamental change. It should also lay out a plan for leveraging the implementation of learner-centered programs through incentives that would encourage such initiatives. For example, to stimulate business participation in the funding of CLC prototypes, the federal government should enact an Education Tax Credit (ETC) allowing corporations to claim tax benefits for their contributions toward CLC construction and related start-up costs, including re-training of teachers as facilitators of self-directed learning. This is discussed further in the section on "State Actions."

Federal tax incentives should also be enacted to encourage philanthropic giving to schools by individuals who fund the start-up of CLCs employing the new learning model.

The federal government should do much more to encourage parental choice, i.e., parents' right to choose the school their children attend, as opposed to the compulsory attendance at the school nearest to their homes. Coupled with a broad CLC initiative, which would greatly increase the numbers of schools available to choose from (a significant problem with the recent federal legislation), this would increase competition among schools and CLCs.

Finally, the federal government, through the Department of Education, should lead the charge by implementing the new learner-centered model in those schools it directly oversees, and it should subsidize state and local programs to construct prototype CLCs.

State Actions

States should not cede authority over education to the federal government, nor should they wait for the federal government to act. Every state can act independently to transform the education system and realize the economic, social, and political benefits of being an early adopter. Each governor should articulate a vision for a learner-centered educational system and should lead statewide and grass-roots efforts to implement that vision.

Transforming education can be the goal around which economic development, urban renewal, and tax savings are organized. The governor should coordinate the policies of all state agencies that play a role in this transformation, including those responsible for education, health, social services, labor, economic development, intergovernmental affairs, and finance.

The centerpiece of a statewide development program to improve education might be a program of state grants for the construction of CLCs in each county or in selected communities and school districts. These state-subsidized CLCs –at least ten in each county – would demonstrate the learner-centered concept to the public, and serve as a resource for training teachers in the new approach. If each of these CLCs spawned two additional CLCs within three years, and then split again within a few years, change would sweep across the entire system within five to seven years, leaving a sufficient number of traditional schools in place to accommodate parents who prefer the old system. By moving to the learner-centered system, significant annual cost savings would be realized in substantially all states. The plan might include state and local tax incentives that would attract local businesses to contribute towards the construction of CLCs and to participate in internship programs with CLCs. A state plan might include a program to influence the federal government to enact a grant and/or income-tax incentive program to mirror the state's plan. However, the availability or timing of federal funds should not be a requirement of the state's plan, nor should the state accept funds that would subject it and individual CLCs to regulations inconsistent with state and local control.

States can take other actions to make sure that the learner-centered approach to education is successfully implemented.

- States should greatly increase parental choice with regard to the schools their children may attend.
- Every state should significantly increase its commitment to charter schools and provide access to capital funds and/or leasing of suitable space and leasehold improvements.
- States should support full utilization of CLCs, including after-school programs, pre-K services, and adult lifelong learning programs.
- States should modify teacher certification regulations to allow qualified candidates to apply for positions as facilitators. Individuals with business experience as "knowledge workers" and retired professionals should be included in facilitator recruitment programs.
- States should declare a moratorium on construction of traditional school structures.
- State laws governing class size should be repealed.

School officials at the state and local level may perceive the transformation of traditional schools into community learning centers as a threat to their existence. They may resist change, seek further centralization, and point to past, failed decentralization efforts. These might include failed approaches, but worthy attempts, such as "site-based management" programs or "community school boards." State and school district leaders must be sensitive to all such barriers to change and provide leadership and incentives to achieve transformation objectives.

The CLC concept goes far beyond previous attempts at reorganization. Coupled with parental choice, CLCs introduce market forces and healthy competition into the process of improving education. Moreover, CLCs represent self-contained, self-organizing systems that fully integrate the learning process and self-governance.

School District or Mayoral Actions

The transformation of the education system on the local level can be a powerful catalyst for reinvigorating the community. School districts or mayors, who often control or influence operation of the schools, should not wait for the federal government or for state governments to act. School districts already have the authority to deliver relevant education services. The school superintendent and the school board do not require permission to transform their educational systems and to institute prototype community learning centers.

The superintendent and school board should conduct their own visioning process to include all staff and the communities they serve. The implementation effort should include several prototype CLCs. Enrollment at the CLCs should be based on the free choice of parents and learners.

Savings generated by school districts shifting from traditional schooling to the CLC model should be applied to reducing taxes and rewarding facilitators for increased productivity. Plans to construct traditional schools should be waived or shelved.

Teacher Actions

By embracing the concept of shared leadership in a CLC, facilitators give up the illusion of authority they may previously have had as teachers in the traditional education system. They go from being at the head of an isolated classroom to having real power as part of a self-organizing team. This allows them to be masters of their own fates, and enables them to realize the professional and financial rewards of being a learning professional in an era in which learning is the source of all wealth.

Teachers and their unions should also play a leading role in transforming the system. Instead of fighting over meager annual increases in salaries and benefits, which barely keep pace with cost-of-living increases, teachers should pressure school district leadership to lift their sights and create a vision of schooling that is appropriate for the Information Age. Teachers should demand a key role in this visioning process and assure that the resulting plans provide for the development of teachers and their empowerment as facilitators for self-directed learners.

If district leadership does not heed the call for transforming the education system, teachers should make the case directly to the community or split from the district and form their own charter schools to implement the new concepts.

College and University Actions

Colleges and universities should recognize that they are following an obsolete learning model and that, eventually, they will suffer a reduction in demand for their brand of traditional academic services. They should also recognize that, collectively, their admission policies indirectly determine the curricula of high schools and, as such, represent a barrier to fundamental change of the education system. To counter these, colleges and universities should themselves launch CLCs and transform themselves into institutions of lifelong learning.

At a minimum, or as an evolutionary step, they should adopt the principles of self-directed learning, establish relationships with K-12 schools and establish or expand apprenticeships and internship programs. Community colleges, which have proven to be innovative and market oriented, and which already serve a wide age group of students, should also implement these changes.

Equally important, teacher colleges should redesign their curricula to emphasize learning-to-learn and facilitation skills. They should open K-12 community learning centers (or form alliances with existing CLCs), and train facilitators through immersion in the CLC approach.

Colleges and universities should encourage their students to volunteer their participation in community learning centers. These students would fulfill a civic responsibility and establish mentoring relationships with CLC learners, while exposing themselves to self-directed learning and programs to enhance learning-to-learn skills.

Business Actions

Business has a great deal at stake in the education system, but business participation in education has been essentially limited to charitable contributions that mainly serve their objectives to recruit college graduates. This tends to reinforce the existing educational system. Instead, business should support systemic change and focus more of its participation on the front-end of education, i.e., kindergarten-through-12th grade.

On this level, business should lend its management expertise to school leaders in order to support their visioning and planning processes for moving to learner-centered education. At the same time, business should participate in the implementation of selected initiatives that will drive fundamental educational change, such as the start-up of prototype community learning centers, facilitator training and internship programs.

Business should consider shifting advertising dollars to investments in public relations campaigns built around their participation in support of K-12 education. For example, partnerships with a school district to start-up a CLC (named for the business that is contributing at least half of capital and start-up costs) will provide real and enduring value to the community, while heightening public appreciation of and employee pride in the business organization.

Business participation in internship programs established with CLCs would provide a further source of value for the community and boost the productivity of learners and the participating businesses. More generally as well, business participation in elementary and secondary education would enhance learner and facilitator appreciation of the interrelationship of capitalism and democracy.

Philanthropist Actions

Philanthropic efforts, however well intentioned, can actually make matters worse by reducing the pressure on schools to make the fundamental changes required for a shift to learner-centered education.

It is crucial for philanthropy to support systemic change in education, rather than subsidizing obsolete methods. It is equally important that greater philanthropic attention be paid to the whole system, including elementary and secondary education.

Philanthropists and charitable foundations have a unique opportunity to make an impact by serving as catalysts for transformational change. Funding the community visioning process and prototype CLCs will serve as the foundation for expansion of learner-centered programs.   Because prototype CLCs will produce savings and spark transformation of the total education system, this will be the gift that keeps on giving.

Parent Actions

Beyond voting in school board elections, parents should be actively involved in their children's school and demand that the schools transform their educational services to meet the needs of the Information Age. They should demand development of community learning centers sufficient to accommodate all those who choose to attend such schools.

Parents should demand the right to send their children to any school in the district. The transformation of traditional schools to CLCs will create many more schools and make meaningful choice a reality.

Parents should participate in the district-wide visioning, planning and implementation phases of the transformation program. The facilitators and learners who are to enroll in the CLCs should participate in the design of their learning programs, constitutions and operating procedures.

Parent associations that support fundamental change and self-directed learning may find that citizen groups who typically vote against school budgets will become allies, once they understand that the new system will cost significantly less than the traditional system.

Parents and learners should receive periodic reports, no less than annually, on the performance of their school districts and their individual schools relative to the adopted budget. These reports should also include a rolling five-year plan to accomplish the vision and related annual goals. The superintendent should seek the counsel of parents, learners, facilitators, and staff in evaluating each school, and the school district as a whole.

Citizen Actions

Every citizen should support political candidates who espouse fundamental change based upon principles of self-directed learning. They should vote against the issuance of bonds to construct traditional schools and, instead, vote for bonds to support the construction of CLCs.

Citizens should take action to increase the consciousness of others in the community who are likely to support change in the local schools. One way to encourage change in the educational system would be for book club members in the community to convince friends to devote reading selections to those about the meaning of the Information Age as it relates to learning and school reform (A list of such books appears in the Bibliography to this book.). Book club members can then carry this effort through to subsequent school board elections, and urge the participants to channel their knowledge about learning and school reform into an increased level of participation in establishing programs and centers for self-directed learning.

Citizens can practice democracy through participation in the school visioning and planning process. If there are none underway, they should urge local officials to start such a process. A suggested plan for starting up a CLC prototype is included in Appendix B.

Conclusion: The Freedom and Responsibility to Innovate

In the Information Age, learning is the "New Frontier." The accelerating pace of change, the world's increasing complexity, and the ongoing knowledge explosion all require fundamental transformation of the education system. The new system must be based on love of learning – which is the foundation of lifelong learning, the mastering of learning-to-learn skills, and finally, on purposeful work.

Correspondingly, the traditional, Machine-Age educational system must go. We must end our reliance on large factory-like schools, prescribed curricula, the segregation of students by age, and the fragmentation of schooling into separate grades, semesters, and 45 to 60 minute class periods.

Indeed, the answer is not "more of the same," as some have erroneously argued. More schooling, more tests, more control, and more efforts to "fix" parts of an obsolete system constitute movement in the wrong direction. These measures will only worsen the passivity of students and will exacerbate the current educational malaise--even if examination scores were to improve under this system. To the contrary, the goal of providing an equal opportunity for all to learn and to succeed will be attained not by efforts to elevate the test scores of poor performers to the mere average, but by helping all children to self-directedly build on their strengths and their natural love of learning in order to realize their full potential.

The new model of learning does this. It vibrantly mirrors the accelerating shift toward empowerment of the modern workforce. Under this model, self-directed learners, assisted by self-organizing teams of facilitators, take responsibility for their learning and their learning environment. This allows self-directed learners to actively participate in all decisions affecting them. Thus, it multiplies their productivity, while enabling a wider understanding of how the world works and a deeper appreciation of democracy.

By contrast, traditional public education has effectively been nothing more than a screening process. Its manifest function has been to separate those deemed suited for the management class from those deemed undeserving of inclusion. In fact, public schools have never really been expected to provide quality service that is responsive to the needs of all students, as they must now do, given the imperatives of the Information Age. And yet, the public schools are the places to initiate revolutionary change, not only because they serve about 90% of our nation's youth, but, more critically, because the public schools provide the broadest opportunity for communities to practice and perfect the ideals of democracy.

If the citizenry and public schools fail to make the needed transition to the new learning model, then the ever-increasing chasm between society's needs and school performance – along with the gap between cost versus value for money in public education – will provide an opening for well-endowed and influential private-sector entrepreneurs and philanthropists to implement the new learning model.

In the end, we in the United States must be guided, as were the Founding Fathers, by our hallowed traditions of individual rights, freedom of expression, and free markets. We, the people, must now reinforce and sustain these traditions. We can do so by designing an education system that allows our youth and the entire citizenry to be responsible for their own development and the shaping of our democracy.

APPENDIX A

FREQUENTLY ASKED QUESTIONS

This appendix can be used by educators, Parent Teacher Association (PTA) members, and citizens to enhance their understanding of the new education system.

Q1. This concept sounds like the "open classroom" movement of the 1960s, which was tried and died out rather quickly. Why try again?

A1. The open classroom initiative was an attempt to address the limitations of the traditional one-teacher model, but it did not empower learners with self-directed learning and a role in school governance. It also did not abolish the graded structure and other elements of the traditional, factory-like model of schooling. The lesson to be learned from the open classroom experience is not that larger groupings of learners are problematic, but that fundamental change to the entire system is necessary, including power-structure changes, such as learner and facilitator empowerment.

Q2. Why establish a community learning center with 12-18 year old learners, rather than kindergarten through high school senior year?

A2. The goal should be to move toward K-12 CLCs. However, during the start-up and transition phase, it is desirable that older learners develop the capacity to work effectively with others, to serve as role models, and to demonstrate the capacity to create value for the community that will spur broader acceptance of the new education system. In the first few years of a CLC start-up, it is preferable to exclude high school juniors and seniors since they are closer to graduation and will lack the commitment to building a learning community.

Q3. Will colleges of choice accept CLC graduates? Will my child's opportunities be limited in any way?

A3. Substantially all of the graduates from the CLC that was established in Alameda, California have enrolled in four-year colleges, including many of the nation's finest.

Graduation from a CLC, where self-directed learning has been practiced, should result in accomplishments that are well-documented and supported by references from facilitators and community leaders. These tangible accomplishments, coupled with the CLC graduate's self-reliance and ability to articulate personal goals, will assure entry into colleges of choice.

Q4. How should facilitators be selected to serve in the CLC?

A4. CLC facilitators should volunteer for appointment to the CLC. Assuming that five facilitators are to staff a CLC, at least two should be relatively new to the teaching profession. This will help assure long-term continuity, provide training benefits, and cost advantages. The selection process should consider the mix of interpersonal and leadership skills, along with subject-matter expertise. Once the facilitator team is established, it should self-select a team leader. The team members should evaluate each other at least annually, which should include in-put from parent/learner surveys. New team members should require a two-thirds vote of the team and the CLC governing board.

Q5. What training does a facilitator require?

A5. Facilitators must be model learners, dedicated to self-directed, lifelong learning. These qualities are considered in the hiring process. Facilitators should read this book and other books listed in the Bibliography. In a start-up situation, the facilitators would benefit from a visitation and a week or two of practicing at an existing CLC or democratic school. New hires at an existing CLC need only observe the facilitation styles of their peers in the CLC, as well as the learners. Facilitators, as lifelong learners, should continually enhance their learning and thinking skills, along with their knowledge in areas useful to the community. This should include, but not be limited to, participation at conferences in order to refresh one's vision. Whether newly established or veteran, facilitators should constantly work on team-building skills. Doing so with a team-building professional is a big plus.

Q6. Why is systems thinking such an important part of the new education system?

A6. Systems thinking looks at a situation or problem in its entirety, rather than in parts, and analyzes the interactions of all relevant variables. It is an important new tool for understanding the complex systems of which we are a part. It is the tool for engaging the collective brainpower of teams and organizations. It will also provide the means for whole-system change that will enable schools to learn, change, and remain relevant. In brief, it will change the way we think, learn, work, organize, and even play.

Q7. The internship component sounds intriguing, but is it feasible and practical?

A7. Yes. Apprenticeship and internship have long been a part of the education system and preparation for the world of work. Now that all work is becoming "knowledge work," apprenticeships and internships can blend academic learning with practical work experience. Also, mentorship is emerging to provide role modeling and counseling. A more meaningful, natural and productive mentoring relationship would arise from the performance of meaningful work by learners desiring to participate in such activities. The rapid development of technology will allow "virtual" apprenticeships and internships to supplement interpersonal activities. There are many examples of youth having skills that are more advanced than that of most adults, such as computer skills. Also, youth bring creativity and fresh perspectives, which will be increasingly valued by business and non-profit organizations. The challenge and the opportunity is to be among the first to forge partnerships with business and non-profit organizations.

Q8. Where do phys-ed and organized sports fit in the new education system?

A8. Self-directed learning honors the individual's right to engage in physical exercise and play sports or games at any time, and for any period of time. However, there would be no requirement for such activities at a CLC. There are those who would be concerned that ending mandatory gym classes or giving learners a choice of when to exercise will result in a worsening of students' physical fitness. They should recognize that allowing such freedom more likely will result in less humiliation, more physical exercise in ways better suited to the child's unique situation, and better lifelong habits of fitness. The smaller size of CLCs would necessitate that learner-athletes seeking to participate in organized team sports affiliate with teams at nearby high schools. Alternatively, they could organize leagues composed of a group of CLCs. Instead of each CLC having its own athletic facilities, the local school district or department of parks would provide a shuttle service to and from a nearby "commons" area.

Q9. Are there any safety issues associated with CLCs?

A9. CLCs, as communities of learners and facilitators who work closely together for six to thirteen years, would be much safer than large, impersonal schools. Unlike the traditional schooling process in which learners compete and are ranked through a grading process, CLCs operate in a cooperative manner in which learners and facilitators get to know each other very well. It is far less likely that learners with serious problems who might pose a threat to the community would go undetected. Small CLCs, located close to home, would eliminate miles-long walks to school by learners who may have to pass through several gang territories, which often results in kids joining gangs as a way of gaining protection. With respect for the learner being paramount and discipline being established through the learner-operated Judicial Committee, the possibility of learners acting out or threatening a facilitator is far less than in a traditional school.

Q10. What is the risk of mixing 12-14 year old girls with much older boys?

A10. The multi-age learning environment is more natural than the traditional, graded structure. Self-directed learners in a CLC are more likely to be excited by learning than in the traditional, competitive and stressful environment. Self-directed learners are treated with respect, and they learn to treat others with respect. Thus, they would form healthy relationships with others at the center. The history of self-directed learning environments has demonstrated that any parental concerns about mixing of the sexes are unfounded. To the contrary, the added self-reliance, self-respect, and self-discipline that flow from self-directed learning serve to enhance overall social skills.

Q11. The state will reduce aid to offset the district's savings from CLCs. Why make the effort to reduce budgets?

A11. The main purpose for changing the education system is not cost savings. The goal is to create self-reliant, effective citizens, capable of participating in democratic decision making. It is also about supporting our youth in their quest to fulfill their personal vision, and to foster equal opportunity for all. If the state is apt to claim all or most of the savings, then the CLCs should pour the savings into capital costs for new CLCs, or make a deal to share the savings with the state, in the same proportion of state aid to local funding.

APPENDIX B

WORKPLAN FOR START-UP OF A COMMUNITY LEARNING CENTER

	Workplan Activity	1	2	3	4	5	6	7	8	9	10	11	12
1	Vision, strategy and CLC proposal to Board of Education	=	=										
2	Board adopts proposal		=										
3	Set up steering committee and Public Benefit Corporation		=										
4	Engage business and foundation sponsors		=										
5	Fundraising	=	=										
6	Develop communication and public relations plan	=	=										
7	Architect plans approved (new construction or re-configuration)	=	=										
8	Enlist community support	=	=	=									
9	Select facilitators	=	=										
10	Program design and development		=	=	=								
11	Establish operating plan		=	=									
12	Complete construction and install CLC learning environment			=	=	=	=						
13	Training for facilitators				=	=	=	=					
14	Develop operating procedures			=	=	=							
15	Install information systems				=	=	=						
16	Conduct marketing for learner enrollment				=	=	=						
17	Design learner orientation program				=	=	=	=					
18	Learner enrollment					=	=	=					
19	Conduct learning program								=	=	=	=	
20	Assessment and improvement								=	=	=	=	
21	Ongoing project management	=	=	=	=	=	=	=	=	=	=	=	=

APPENDIX C

PROPOSAL FOR A COMMUNITY LEARNING CENTER

This appendix can serve as an illustrative guide for a group of founders of a Community Learning Center to use in preparing a proposal for a charter school to the School Board.

INTRODUCTION AND SUMMARY
- Legal entity to be established
- Students to be served; ages, enrollment, and community
- Vision overview
- Relationship to School District
- Location of CLC
- Capital funding sources
- Operating funding sources
- Sustainability issues

LEARNING PROGRAM
PRINCIPLES OF LEARNING
- Love of learning is the foundation of lifelong learning.
- Learners pursue a personal vision and their personal learning plans.
- Self-directed learning flows from learners' rights, dignity and freedom.
- Learners are responsible for their own learning, which is self-paced.
- Self-directed learning includes self-assessment.
- Learners have an equal voice in all decisions that affect them.
- Learners administer the judicial and disciplinary process.
- Teachers are facilitators of learner-directed learning; model learners.
- Multi-age groupings replace traditional grade structure.
- Learning-to-learn skills, including teamwork, are encouraged; breadth of knowledge in science, math, social studies, etc., are acquired as a by-product of acquiring learning-to-learn skills.
- Systems thinking skills are encouraged.

- Computer modeling skills are encouraged.
- The arts, music and creativity are encouraged.
- Learners are responsible for custodial and administrative functions.
- Learners are responsible for participating in the facilitation of others' learning.
- Learners are exposed to several career paths through quality internships.
- Learners earn a diploma upon demonstrating effective citizenship.

CURRICULUM DESIGN AND PROGRAMS

- Learners develop personal learning plans and, with facilitator support, develop goals for the CLC.
- Learners, with facilitator support, design the learning program for the CLC.
- Learners and facilitators design, develop and conduct learning-to-learn seminars.
- Learners and facilitators design, develop and conduct systems thinking seminars.
- Learners form teams, clubs, and corporations to pursue common goals.
- Learners participate in solving a variety of community problems.
- Learners lead programs to facilitate learning of K-5 learners.
- Learners participate in a variety of internship programs (off campus and virtual).
- Learners participate in college level courses, including on-line courses.
- Learners obtain feedback from users of their services, peers, and facilitators.
- Learners participate in learning competitions, such as FIRST (science & tech).
- Learners participate in performing arts programs.
- Learners participate in sports programs.
- Learners self-test and prep for state exams and college entrance exams.

- Learners prepare portfolios to document their learning relative to goals.
- Learners evaluate the performance of the CLC.

LEARNER ASSESSMENTS AND FEEDBACK
- Peer feedback on learners' contributions, learner-led seminars, etc.
- User assessment of learners' internship accomplishments
- User assessment of learners' custodial and administrative activities
- Facilitator assessment of learner-led seminars and K-5 facilitation
- Parent and facilitator assessment of progress against personal learning plan
- Performance on college, state, and school district exams
- Community feedback on Graduate Profile and presentation for diploma

CLC PERFORMANCE MEASURES
- Learner satisfaction
- Parent satisfaction
- Graduation and drop-out rates
- College acceptances and proportion of first choices
- Accomplishments of graduates
- Internship sponsors satisfaction
- Frequency of democratic decision making
- Learner performance on state exams, SATs, etc.
- Performance gaps and progress in closing them

GOVERNANCE STRUCTURE
- Board of trustees and committees thereof (learners chair each committee)
  - Personnel
  - Standards
  - Financial management and budget
  - Learning program
  - Program evaluation
- Annual meeting of CLC Assembly and selection of Trustees

- Weekly meeting of school community, chaired by a learner
- Leadership committee, chaired by lead facilitator
- Decision making process
- Administrative process

EMPLOYMENT QUALIFICATIONS

- Standards and procedures for engaging and compensating facilitators
- Standards for involving parents and community members
- Standards for engaging and compensating non-certified personnel

HEALTH AND SAFETY

- Behavioral rules, compliance and enforcement procedures
- Plant safety, fire safety, electrical and other risk management issues
- Off-site risks, including internships
- Risks to learners due to harassment of any type
- Health risks and related emergencies
- Special education students
- Criminal record checks for all employees and volunteers

ADMISSION POLICIES

- Commitment to equal opportunity and representation of the community
- Targeted marketing to achieve balance and assure minority representation
- Enrollment procedures and application process
- Lottery to deal with applications in excess of openings
- Sibling preferences
- Out-of-district applicants
- Interview procedure
- Acceptance procedure and confirmation process
- Disciplinary procedures, including suspensions and expulsions

OTHER ISSUES
- Right of return of charter employees
- Dispute resolution procedures
- Amendment to the charter
- Manner in which administrative procedures will be provided
- Statewide standards and pupil assessment
- Budget for first three years

APPENDIX D

POTENTIAL ANNUAL SAVINGS IN K-12 PUBLIC SCHOOLS

The following table, which utilizes data for the 2002 school year, shows the potential annual cost savings from transforming the U.S. public school system to a self-directed learning system, which will cost an average of $5,940 per pupil. As important as these savings are, the more important benefits are the strengthening of democracy, the increased relevance of the new system, the ability of the new system to anticipate and adapt to change and the equality of opportunity that would be achieved.

State	Students	Spending (Billions)	Spending Per-Pupil 2002	Per-Pupil Savings	Annual Savings (Billions)
United States	47,575,862	$357.955	$7,524	$1,584	$75.360
Alabama	726,367	4.312	5,937	(3)	(0.002)
Alaska	134,023	1.264	9,430	3,490	0.468
Arizona	903,518	4.920	5,445	(495)	(0.447)
Arkansas	448,246	2.584	5,764	(176)	(0.079)
California	6,247,889	42.973	6,878	938	5.861
Colorado	742,065	4.634	6,244	304	0.226
Connecticut	570,145	5.996	10,517	4,577	2.610
Delaware	115,486	1.110	9,612	3,672	0.424
D.C.	68,449	0.754	11,009	5,069	0.347
Florida	2,500,161	15.582	6,232	292	0.730
Georgia	1,470,634	11.225	7,633	1,693	2.490
Hawaii	184,546	1.250	6,775	835	0.154
Idaho	246,000	1.424	5,789	(151)	(0.037)
Illinois	2,068,182	15.713	7,598	1,658	3.429
Indiana	994,545	7.990	8,034	2,094	2.083
Iowa	491,169	3.500	7,126	1,186	0.583
Kansas	468,140	3.233	6,906	966	0.452
Kentucky	630,461	4.066	6,449	509	0.321
Louisiana	731,474	4.586	6,270	330	0.241
Maine	211,461	1.725	8,160	2,220	0.469
Maryland	860,890	6.755	7,847	1,907	1.642
Massachusetts	979,593	9.682	9,883	3,943	3.863
Michigan	1,733,900	14.930	8,611	2,671	4.631
Minnesota	845,700	6.623	7,832	1,892	1.600
Mississippi	491,686	2.574	5,235	(705)	(0.347)
Missouri	892,582	5.868	6,574	634	0.566
Montana	151,970	1.076	7,080	1,140	0.173

State	Students	Spending (Billions)	Spending Per-Pupil 2002	Per-Pupil Savings	Annual Savings (Billions)
Nebraska	285,022	2.151	7,547	1,607	0.458
Nevada	356,038	2.184	6,134	194	0.069
New Hampshire	211,429	1.676	7,926	1,986	0.420
New Jersey	1,380,502	13.248	9,596	3,656	5.047
New Mexico	316,143	2.242	7,093	1,153	0.365
New York	2,920,000	31.317	10,725	4,785	13.972
North Carolina	1,303,928	8.577	6,578	638	0.832
North Dakota	106,047	0.655	6,173	233	0.025
Ohio	1,808,000	15.020	8,308	2,368	4.281
Oklahoma	620,404	3.837	6,184	244	0.151
Oregon	552,144	4.572	8,280	2,340	1.292
Pennsylvania	1,810,390	15.701	8,673	2,733	4.948
Rhode Island	157,599	1.610	10,216	4,276	0.674
South Carolina	648,000	4.652	7,179	1,239	0.803
South Dakota	126,560	0.815	6,442	502	0.064
Tennessee	938,162	5.132	5,470	(470)	(0.441)
Texas	4,128,429	28.208	6,833	893	3.687
Utah	477,801	2.279	4,769	(1,171)	(0.560)
Vermont	99,599	0.976	9,798	3,858	0.384
Virginia	1,162,780	8.665	7,452	1,512	1.758
Washington	1,009,626	7.306	7,236	1,296	1.308
West Virginia	281,400	2.460	8,742	2,802	0.788
Wisconsin	878,809	7.605	8,654	2,714	2.385
Wyoming	87,768	0.720	8,203	2,263	0.199

NOTES

1. **SOURCE OF DATA** for the traditional system is the U.S. Department of Education. The amounts represent the estimates provided by state departments of education. The per-pupil annual cost for the new education system is derived from the sample budget displayed in the section of this book entitled "Breakthrough Quality at Lower Cost."

2. **THE POTENTIAL SAVINGS OF APPROXIMATELY $75 BILLION PER YEAR,** which represents a reduction of approximately 20%, assumes that the entire system was transformed and that all traditional schools were replaced by Community Learning Centers.

3. **LARGER COST SAVINGS AND SOCIETAL BENEFITS** would be derived from increased workforce productivity and reductions in welfare, crime, etc.

APPENDIX E

DYNAMIC SCORING™: THE SYSTEMS THINKING PROCESS FOR DESIGNING AND ASSESSING COMMUNITY LEARNING CENTERS

Among the barriers to "whole-system" change is the tendency to focus on selected parts of the educational system, such as class size or the size of the high school, and to "fix" them. However, systems thinking and Dynamic Scoring™ seek to understand the entire system at the structural level, along with the interaction of its parts, as a basis for redesigning the system as a whole. As described in this book, systems thinking and Dynamic Scoring are new tools for thinking, learning-to-learn, and assessment. They are integral parts of the new curricula that can be used to construct a shared understanding of the education system as it currently exists and as the learning community wishes it to be.

This appendix applies the concepts of systems thinking and Dynamic Scoring to graphically illustrate how the key variables of the education system interact to produce the structure of the learning system that we seek to create. The system is illustrated here by using a causal loop diagram (CLD), which is "built up" in a series of charts.

The CLD, typically the result of collaborative effort by representatives from throughout an organization, is a systems thinking tool that facilitates a shared understanding of the entire system. It may serve as the foundation for developing a computer model to test the validity of assumptions and to play out alternative courses of action. It may also be used as an input to the organization's performance measurement process. As such, it is part of the new accounting model, Dynamic Scoring, developed by the author of this book, used in planning for alternative futures, assessing progress toward the vision, and sharing information with all stakeholder groups.

The CLD explicitly describes the cause-effect relationships that form the "structure" or "framework" of the system. The advantage of a causal loop diagram is that it shows how all of the important key factors, or variables, are linked together in a "systems map." In addition, it allows the discovery of feed-

Chart 1: Reinforcing feedback loop producing a "snowball effect"

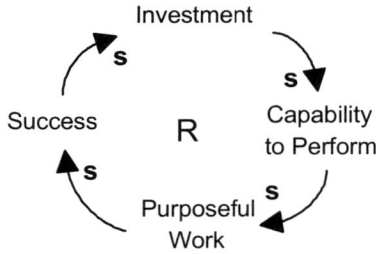

Investment

S

Success   R   Capability
                  to Perform

S   S

Purposeful
Work

S

Chart 2: A reinforcing feedback loop produces both positive and negative exponential growth

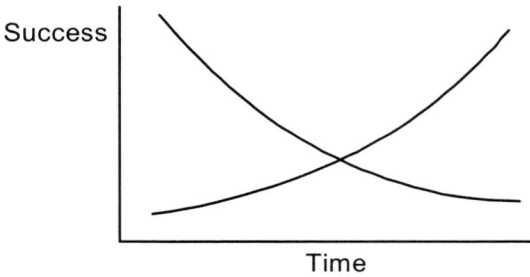

Success

Time

Chart 3: A balancing feedback loop produces stability

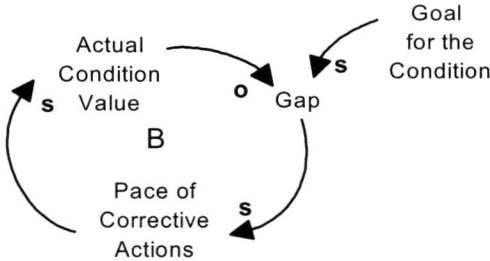

Goal
for the
Condition

Actual
Condition
Value   o   Gap   S

S

B

Pace of
Corrective   S
Actions

Chart 4: A balancing feedback loop generates goal-seeking behavior

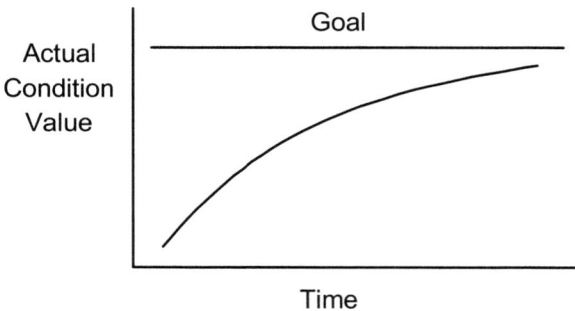

Goal

Actual
Condition
Value

Time

back relationships that are the structural source of all dynamic behavior within complex social and economic systems.

Before we delve into our map of the educational system, an understanding of causal loop diagrams will be useful. There are two basic types of causal loop structures. The first is a reinforcing feedback loop, as illustrated in **Chart 1**. This structure seeks to generate exponential change in the variables that are included in the loop and is the source of the patterns of behavior we commonly refer to as a "snowball effect" or "increasing returns" or, when moving in a negative direction, a "vicious cycle." Thus, **Chart 2**, which shows both positive and negative exponential growth, illustrates the patterns of behavior associated with the reinforcing feedback loop. Reinforcing feedback strives to accelerate exponential change.

The balancing feedback loop, illustrated in **Chart 3**, generates patterns of behavior that seek either an explicit or implicit "goal." Balancing feedback provides stability to a system. **Chart 4** presents an example of such goal-seeking behavior.

As seen in the examples, the factors, or variables, in a feedback loop are connected by single direction arrows called causal links. The cause variable is at the tail of the arrow, and the effect variable is at the head of the arrow. An "o" at the head means the cause and effect move in "opposite" directions. Otherwise the cause and the effect move in the same direction. Sometimes an "s" is placed at the head to more explicitly indicate that the cause and effect move in the same direction. A feedback loop occurs whenever the causal links form a pathway that leads back to the variable that was selected as the starting point. A single variable could be part of many feedback loops. A feedback loop is "balancing" if there is an odd number of "o's" in the loop. Otherwise, it is a reinforcing loop.

The goal we are seeking for learning in the 21st Century is an ever-increasing community of learners. **Chart 5,** on the next page, illustrates the objective of our efforts to transform education: an exponential growth in the quality and quantity of education and learning communities.

Chart 5: The goal is exponential growth in the Community of Learners

**Quantity and Quality of a
Community of Learners**

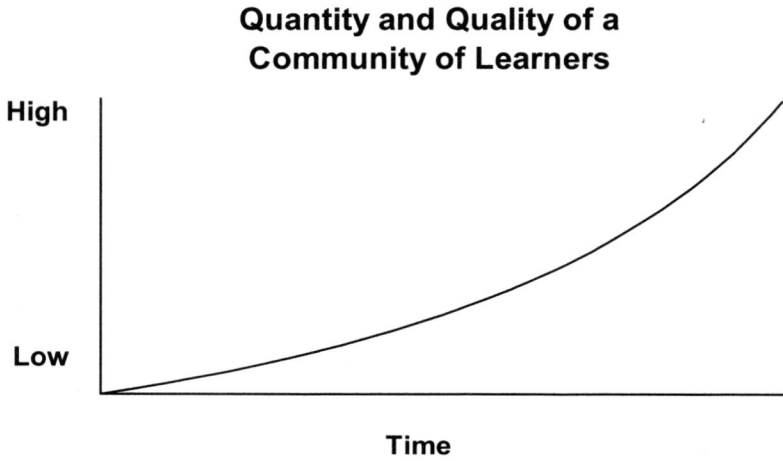

High

Low

Time

Thus, in our systems map, we represent our goal by the phrase, *A Learning Community*. This is the goal of our journey of discovery. The CLD describes the pathways that together form the reinforcing feedback structures that will achieve that aim.

The phrase "community" suggests a group of people having common interests. In a learning community, the shared interest is a lifelong desire to learn and to share knowledge for the benefit of everyone. Personal learning, thus, is demonstrated and becomes part of the community's organizational knowledge.

There are several "stakeholders" in a learning community. They are of all ages and engage in the full range of occupations and professions. In this community, the capacity to create value from knowledge matters deeply to each stakeholder, either as an individual or as a member of a specific sub-group.

There are very specific, and often very personal, expectations that these stakeholders have for the institutions they create and sustain to develop and distribute knowledge. There are, however, some common expectations for the institutions that make up the community's "education system," which has accountability for developing the capability of students to learn. We believe there are at least three important, commonly shared stakeholder expectations. They are as follows:

- Students should succeed in school, and should expect that success in school will help generate a rewarding post-school career.
- Professionals who deliver educational services will perform with high quality at the lowest cost possible.
- All students in the community will have equitable access to educational resources of the community.

Later in this appendix, we develop how these stakeholder expectations can work to generate positive change for our educational institutions.

The accelerating pace of change is a new reality that requires a fundamental shift from teaching a prescribed body of knowledge to a process of learning-to-learn and to a system that nurtures love of learning, which is essential for lifelong learning. Rather than "covering the curricula," it is "uncovered"

Chart 6: A Learning Community as the effects of Self-directed Learning and Democratic Decision Making

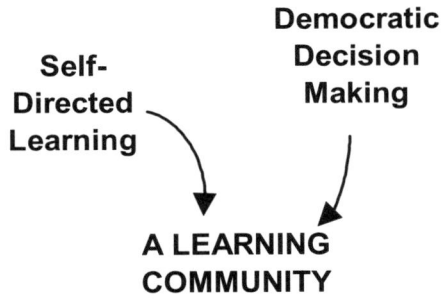

Self-
Directed
Learning

Democratic
Decision
Making

A LEARNING
COMMUNITY

through a discovery process, based on the natural, self-directed way of learning that everyone is born with. We must migrate from a system of teachers, educators, and students to one of learners responsible for their own learning, with a facilitator's support and counsel.

A major barrier to self-directed learning is the lock-step grade structure of elementary and secondary schools that groups students by age and moves them along in assembly-line fashion, ignoring the differences in style and pace of learning. Compounding the problem is the fragmenting of time by dividing the school day into 45-60 minute periods. By ending the rigid program of hourly periods for a multi-age grouping (ages 12-18) students are allowed to learn at their own pace and to immerse themselves in areas of interest, which are the key ingredients for highly effective, even spectacular *Self-Directed Learning.*

In **Chart 6**, the causal link from self-directed learning to the learning community means that as the quality of self-directed learning increases, the quality of the learning community will also increase. Similarly, the quality of the learning community will decline if the quality of self-directed learning decreases or does not exist.

Another characteristic of a learning community is *Democratic Decision Making.* The capability of a student to successfully pursue self-directed learning depends greatly on the operating policies and scheduling practices of the school. Therefore, the effective pursuit of self-directed learning suggests that students should have a vote in all of the important institutional decisions that affect their lives and their work at school. This assumption is represented by the causal link in **Chart 7,** on the next page, between democratic decision making and self-directed learning on the diagram. It means that democratic decision making (the cause) and self directed learning (the effect) move in the same direction.

Participation in the decision making processes of the school not only creates a foundation for genuine self-directed learning; it also represents a wonderful learning opportunity. Beyond exposure to decision making itself, it exposes the students to current real-world issues, allows them to interact with others and adds considerably to their understanding of the relevance of their school work.

Chart 7: The influences of Democratic Decision Making, Stewardship by Students, and Empowerment of Local School Sites on Self-Directed Learning and a Learning Community.

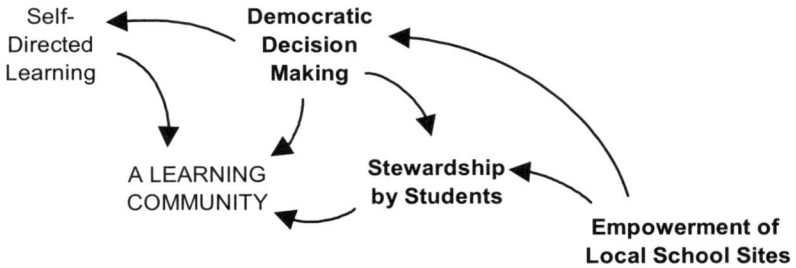

In centers with multi-age groupings of 150 students (ages 12-18), 25 students leave and 25 enter each year. This makes the center a "living system." Students have reason to care about *their* school, which will live forever if it continually improves and is periodically re-designed. The students are motivated to participate directly in the school improvement process and become "stewards" of the school.

Activities, which demonstrate **Stewardship by Students** of their school, may take the form of older students serving as teacher-aides in the elementary school, participating in custodial functions and in the various administrative functions, including assessment of the school's performance and reporting to stakeholders. These activities create tremendous learning opportunities for students.

However, enthusiastic behavior by students as stewards and meaningful, responsible student governance cannot occur without systemic change that results in the **Empowerment of Local School Sites**.

The innovation that must occur within each school location cannot occur without trusting that the students and leaders on-site will decide and act in the best interests of their community. We must be willing to allow the members of the schools to learn from the consequences of their free choices.

Real empowerment of local schools will require **Supportive Changes in Public Policy** that will alter the fundamental authority structures governing schools. By that we mean answering the question: "Who decides?" Such public policies might include programs to encourage parental choice of schools, including vouchers, which would promote diversity and equity. They might also include alternative learning philosophies and methods, such as charter schools and at-home schooling.

However, there are deep-seated **Attitudinal Barriers to Transformation** of the school system. One powerful entrenched barrier is the fear of change that would affect, for example, the number of jobs, how value will be measured, and the kind of organizational and individual values to be emphasized and rewarded.

Chart 8: Stakeholder Pressure for Change, which can lead to Supportive Changes in Public Policy, must overcome the influences of Attitudinal Barriers to Transformation if local school sites are to become successfully empowered.

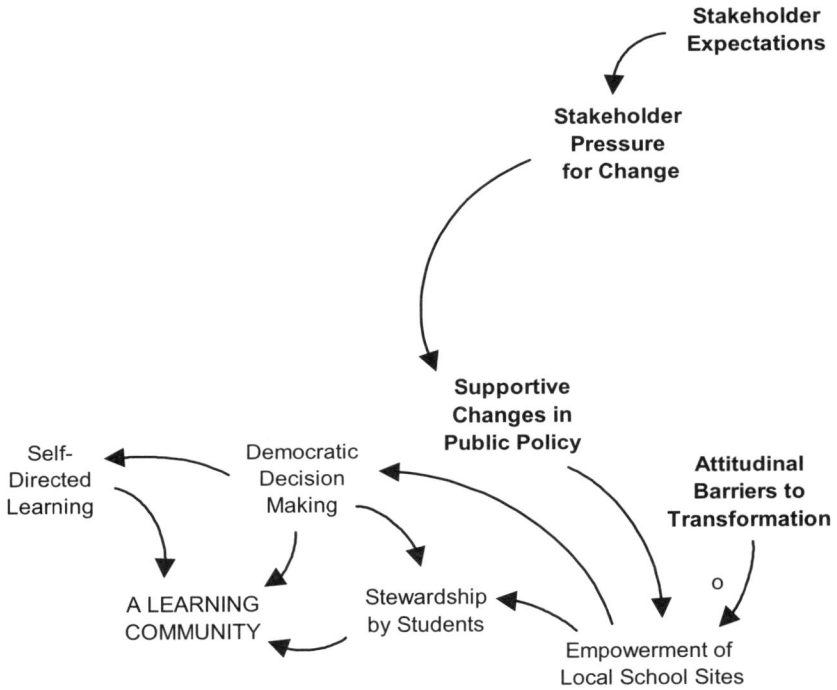

Notice that, in **Chart 8**, the link from attitudinal barriers to empowerment of local schools has an "o" next to the arrowhead. This means that the cause has an effect in the opposite direction. In this instance, it conveys the idea that for empowerment to increase, attitudinal barriers must be decreased.

Earlier, we suggested that a learning community is comprised of stakeholders who have a shared interest in the effectiveness of learning and the utilization of knowledge. These shared interests are the sources for *Stakeholder Expectations.*

To "expect" something is to look forward to its probable occurrence or appearance; to consider it likely or certain; and to consider it obligatory or required. An "expectation" is not to be taken lightly. A system "condition" that is expected does not exist *today*, but it is assumed that it will exist *tomorrow*! Thus, stakeholder expectations are the cause of *Stakeholder Pressure for Change*. The source of this pressure is the *tension* that exists between the desired condition (the expectation) and the "actual" condition of something that is important to the stakeholder. Stakeholder pressure for change often produces supportive changes in public policy.

As mentioned above, there are at least three important, commonly held stakeholder expectations. The first is that students should succeed in school, and that success in school will help generate a rewarding post-school career. The second is that the professionals who deliver educational services will perform at high quality, at the lowest cost possible. The third expectation is that all students in the community will have equitable access to educational resources of the community.

Chart 9: An Attractive, Valid, Compelling Vision is essential for making the case for change in the education system.

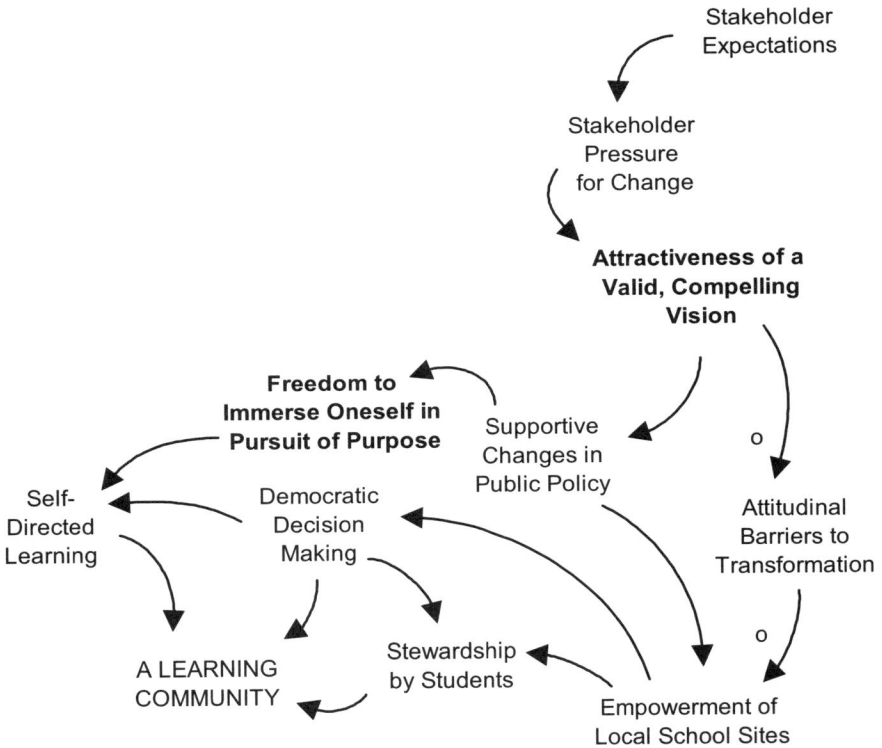

Note: The success of Self-Directed Learning depends upon learners having the freedom to immerse themselves in the pursuit of purpose.

The ***Attractiveness of a Valid, Compelling Vision***, shown in **Chart 9**, is essential in making the case for change. It must be so powerful that it causes people to want to run to this new place – to set aside their fear of change and to embrace the future that results from change. It must resonate with the values they hold most dearly. And, of course, it must include the achievement of stakeholder expectations. This relationship is represented by the causal link to the Compelling Vision variable from Stakeholder Pressure for Change. The more the vision recognizes and validates the expectations of the community's stakeholders, the more attractive it will be to them. Thus, a compelling vision is a powerful force for change.

Let's re-cap where we are on our systems map. We have described both a theory and some concrete suggestions for creating two of the essential attributes of a vital learning community: the first of these is democratic decision making that enables self-directed learning to occur and the second is the sense of stewardship by students for their school. We have argued that a compelling, attractive vision for the future of public education is a necessary condition for these patterns of behavior to occur. But there is more to the story.

The success of self-directed learning depends on the student's ***Freedom to Immerse Oneself in the Pursuit of Purpose***, which provides a personalized meaning to the discovery or creation of knowledge. For learning in the 21st century, this suggests that the student, with a facilitator's support and counsel, will develop a self-directed learning program. This requires freedom to construct the program in a way that may not conform to a pre-determined schedule of standardized achievement tests. Obtaining this scheduling flexibility will, most likely, require supportive changes in public policy—changes that run counter to an accelerating public desire for a prescribed and more quantifiable set of common compliance standards. Yet, because we are convinced that self-directed learning is essential to our learning community, it is important that public policy not constrain the freedom of students to create meaning in their work.

But, to maximize the opportunities for effective and efficient self-directed learning, public policy initiatives need to do more than simply remove obstacles. The most supportive

Chart 10: Public policy, which enables the acquisition and use of Technology to Support Learning Skills, is another key cause Self-Directed Learning.

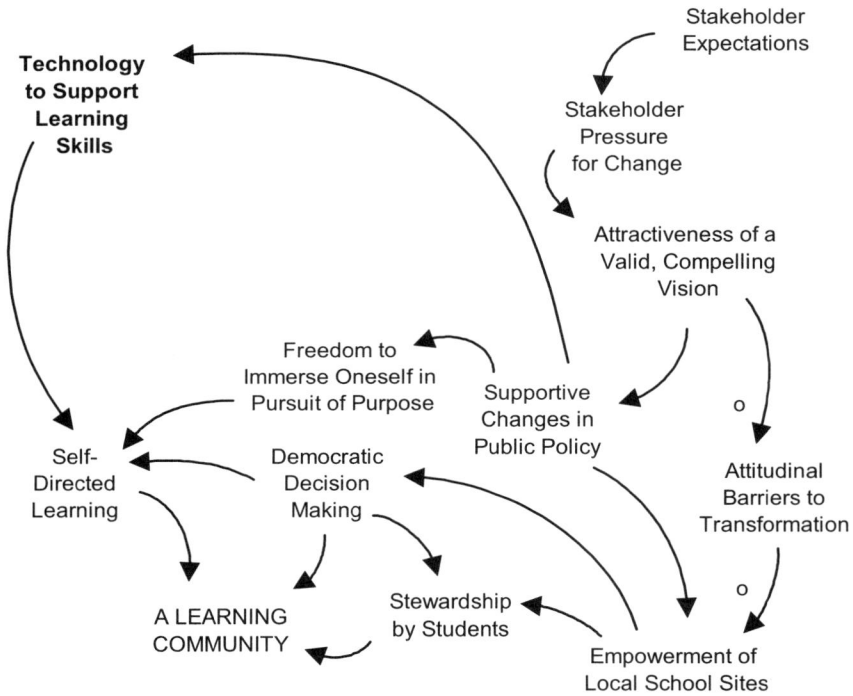

changes in public policy will lead to a significant increase in funding that is aimed at stimulating the development and deployment of *Technology to Support Learning Skills,* as shown in **Chart 10**.

Central governments, in particular, have the opportunity to fund R&D for the creation of effective learning tools and methods in the same way that central resources are used to support basic research in a number of other industries.

Fortunately, government funding is not the only source of investment to develop innovative learning tools and methods. Many private companies have realized the market and profit potential for helping students improve their capability to learn. We can look forward to productive competition in this arena.

However, economic benefits from the implementation of information technology to improve operational effectiveness within schools and associated administrative functions are not easily achieved. Most often, a single school district lacks the size to justify the cost of such extensive installations. For many of these school districts, the most productive avenue is to outsource their information processing functions to private firms. These firms provide technical competence and economies of scale by being able to serve a number of school districts from a single service center.

An emerging issue is the uneven access to technology by students. We are likely to see government policies that increase the availability of computers and Internet access to low-income segments of the population.

The accelerated pace of change and societal pressures generate tremendous stress on the teachers in our schools. Teachers need public support, at both personal and public policy levels. Individually, they deserve the gratitude and admiration of the learners and the communities they support.

At a system-wide level, they need supportive changes in public policy that will enable a better return for the investment in teacher development, teacher recruiting, and the retention of high-performance teachers. The current "model" for teacher effectiveness within our current school systems has become obsolete and counterproductive.

Chart 11: Innovative Teacher Development and Recruiting, which values and encourages Self-Directed Learning and the use of Technology to Support Learning Skills, will develop people who can deliver Effective Facilitation of Learning Productivity.

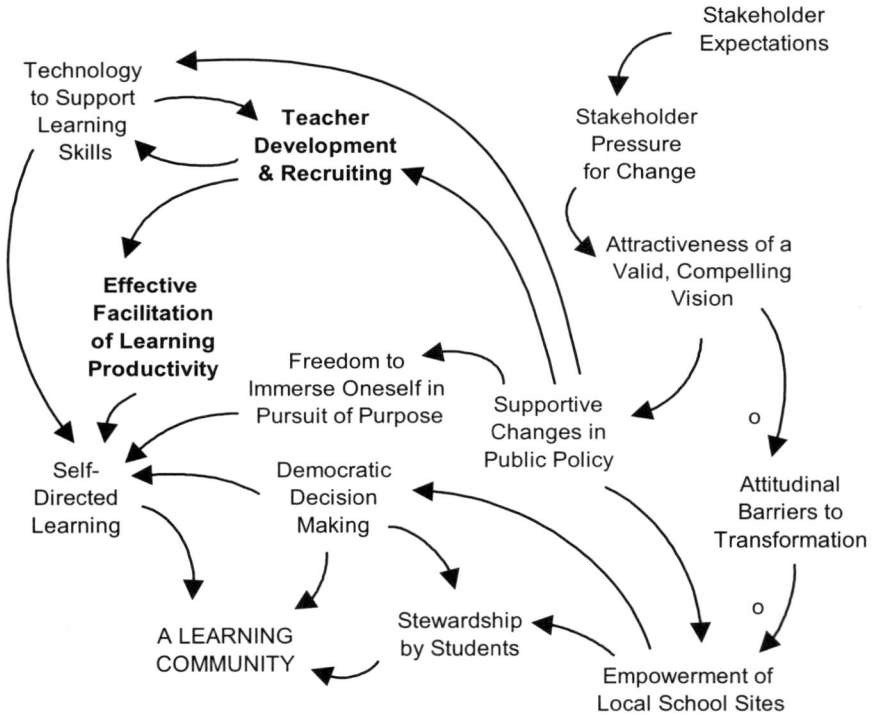

In schools of the future, teachers will – for the most part – be facilitators of self-directed learning. As shown in **Chart 11**, this desired outcome means more effective and innovative ***Teacher Development and Recruitment*** will be a consequence of supportive changes in public policy.

For our present schools and their teachers, there is both good and bad news. The bad news is that the demand for teachers in the next decade will be greater than ever before due to retirement of almost half of the teachers in our schools today. The good news is that schools will still have the opportunity to recruit and develop teachers with new, enhanced skills that can meet the needs for learning in the 21st century. This means that there is now the opportunity to re-tool our current and new teachers to enable them to be the primary providers of ***Effective Facilitation of Learning Productivity,*** which is also shown in Chart 11.

Learning productivity is the ratio of the amount of *learner knowledge produced* per the unit of *effort expended* by learners and facilitators. Each school can establish its own method of defining and measuring learning productivity, but, in almost every case, teachers are the persons who are assigned to facilitate the student's growth in learning productivity. This requires that teachers help students achieve competency in the following capabilities:

- Acquiring new knowledge
- The use of technology to support learning skills
- Learning-to-learn skills, including systems thinking skills
- Self-assessment of learning
- Clarity in the pursuit of purpose
- Democratic decision making
- Personal mastery through teaching
- Purposeful work in the community
- Their roles as members of a learning community

Chart 12: Investment in Community Learning Centers creates the essential learning environment, including physical and governance structures, and enables the Effective Facilitation of Learning Productivity.

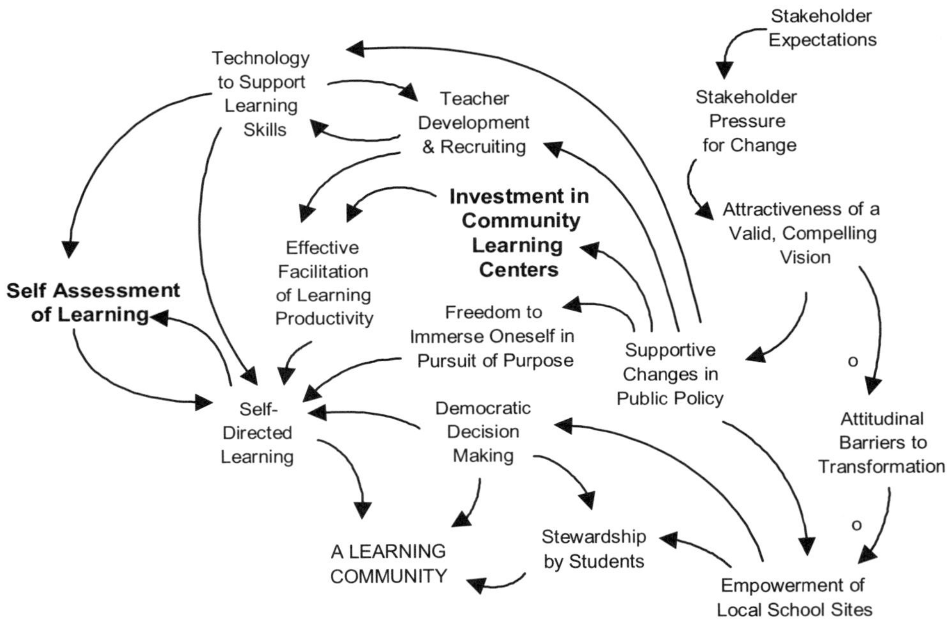

The consequences of the more effective facilitation of learning productivity by teachers are a significant increase in self-directed learning and the resultant favorable impact that it has throughout the education system described here.

A community's *Investment in Community Learning Centers* can dramatically enhance the effective facilitation of learning productivity by skillful teachers. Facilitators and learners must be provided with the physical and governance structures that create an essential environment for self-directed learning. Teams of learners follow different pathways, thus creating unique competencies that allow learners to interact and enhance continuous learning.

Not only can innovative technology be used to enhance learning skills, but, as shown in **Chart 12,** we can also expect information and communication technology to strengthen the learner's capability for *Self Assessment of Learning* to examine objectively the pace, content, and quality of his or her learning.
In industry, self-assessment is called "benchmarking." There, it involves contrasting the performance outcomes from a set of business activities to Global Best Practices in order to determine what process improvements need to be made. In education, we expect that, with complementary technological resources, individual students will be able to communicate with a peer group engaged in the self-directed, purposeful pursuit of knowledge anywhere in the world.

As noted earlier, the systems thinking discipline requires that we become acutely aware of feedback relationships. In our theory of learning, there is a powerful reinforcing feedback loop between self-directed learning and self-assessment. More effective and skillful self-assessment will lead to more focused, meaningful learning. Improving one will lead to an improvement in the other. Diminish one, and the other will also be lessened. The reinforcing feedback relationship between these two key factors is, ultimately, the most essential and powerful source of a student's success.

The accelerating pace of change and rapid obsolescence of knowledge requires a fundamental change from a learning theory based upon knowledge transfer to one based on knowledge creation and an emphasis on *Learning-to-learn,* as

Chart 13: Learning-to-Learn skills, reinforced and enlivened by technology, and including self-assessment training, strengthen both elements of the Self-Directed Learning and Self-Assessment reinforcing feedback loop.

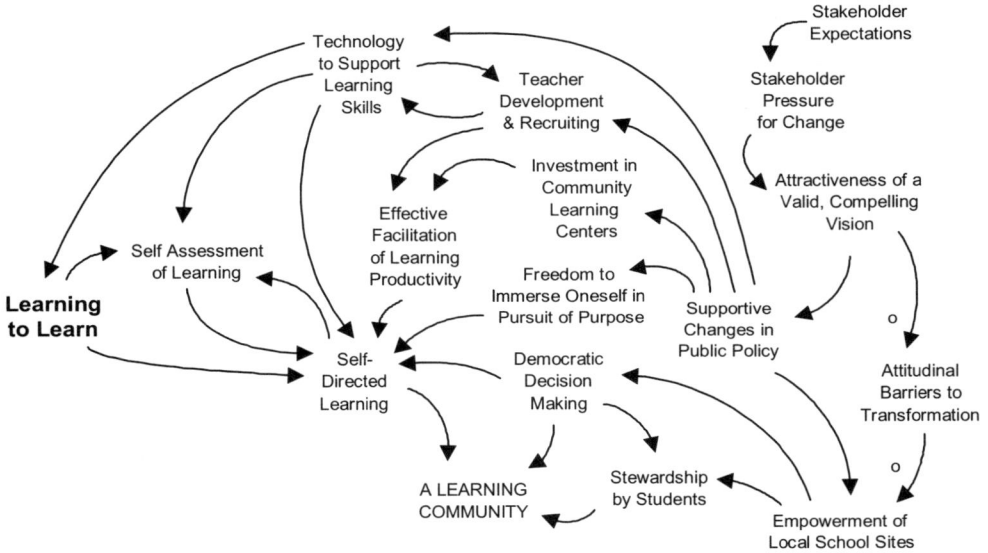

illustrated in **Chart 13**.

Self-directed learning is strengthened by providing students with an opportunity to master selected basic learning skills early in their formal schooling. An intensive "learning-to-learn" program of several months should be available to all students to help them acquire foundation skills in such areas as theory of knowledge, strategic reading, effective writing, research, note-taking, effective presentations, teamwork, systems thinking, facilitation, self-assessment, work organization, and the use of computers. In the typical school of today, these skills are either provided as specialty courses late in the student's career, or are assumed to be imparted by osmosis, as a by-product of the regular curricula. But they are not evaluated separately and are, therefore, not effectively taught or learned. In a world of accelerating change, where these basic skills are as important as core knowledge, all students should acquire them as early as possible. This will enable students to greatly improve their learning and assessment capabilities throughout their school years and their later lives.

But, given the demands on schools today, where will the time for learning and mastering the new basics come from? The love of learning that follows from self-directed learning will shift much of the 28 hours per week now spent on TV to self-motivated learning and school-based activities. It is also likely that apprenticeship to schools, business and community will incorporate the new basics and provide on-the-job training and development. But, most significantly, these learning-to-learn skills will greatly increase learner productivity and thereby increase in-school time available for learning the new basics.

Supportive changes in public policy, especially when expressed by funding to develop innovative high-tech and low-tech teaching tools and methods, are important to enhancing our students' capability to learn how to learn. For this reason, the causal link is shown in Chart 13 as extending from the variable Technology to Support Learning Skills to the Learning-to-learn variable.

Chart 14: Learners are motivated to master the knowledge that they share with their peers, and are asked to teach to others.

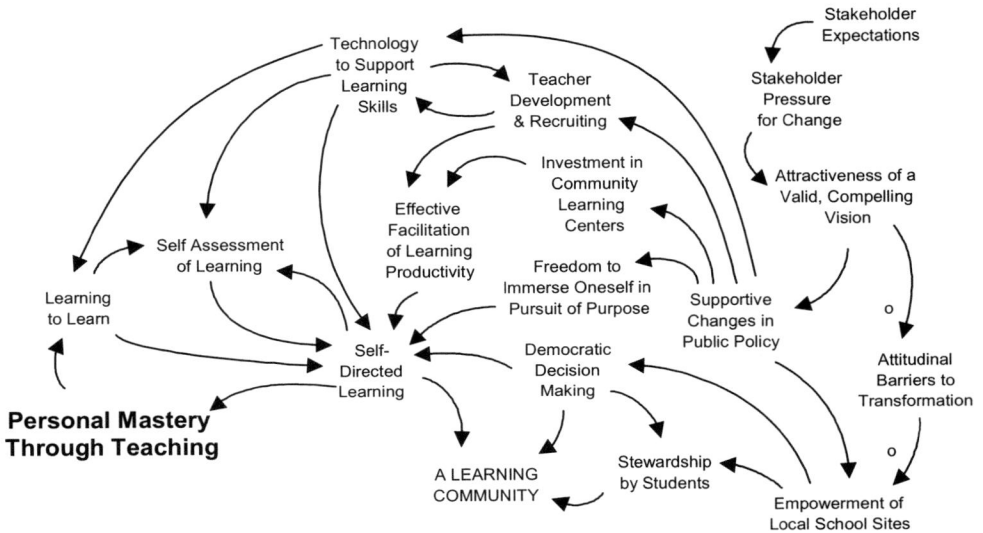

A student's natural desire to learn, when allowed to reach fulfillment through self-direction and self-assessment, creates a level of excitement about knowledge that, for many, must be shared. The student becomes a teacher!

In our vision of learning for the 21st century, older students will serve as supplemental teachers and peer tutors, with a special mission of helping younger students get an early, successful start at acquiring the lifelong learning skills they will need. By empowering students to help teach, not only will schools gain a valuable resource at no added cost, but students also will gain the sense of ***Personal Mastery Through Teaching,*** as shown in **Chart 14.** They will need this sense for the dynamic workplace they will encounter upon graduation, along with thinking, working and people skills that will give them real self-esteem.

A good analogy to reinforce this point is the one-room schoolhouse of the American frontier, which typically accommodated a wide array of students of varying ages and talents. Rather than treating the students as identical passive units – which the schools typically do today – the teachers largely relied on the students both to teach themselves and to help each other learn. By learning to teach, students also "learned to learn" in a manner that prepared them for the real world.

Note that the causal link from Personal Mastery through Teaching to Learning-to-Learn has formed another feedback loop, including self-directed learning. This means that if any one of the variables in this feedback loop is increased, then we have started a "snowball" or "increasing returns" effect. On the other hand, if any of these factors is diminished, then the consequence will be a "vicious cycle" that will diminish, over time, each of the other variables. This is both the power and the danger of a reinforcing feedback structure.

Chart 15: When students, through effective internships and apprenticeships, perform Purposeful Work in the Community, Students' Knowledge grows exponentially due to a strong reinforcing feedback loop. A natural effect of Purposeful Work is the Pursuit of Lifelong Learning.

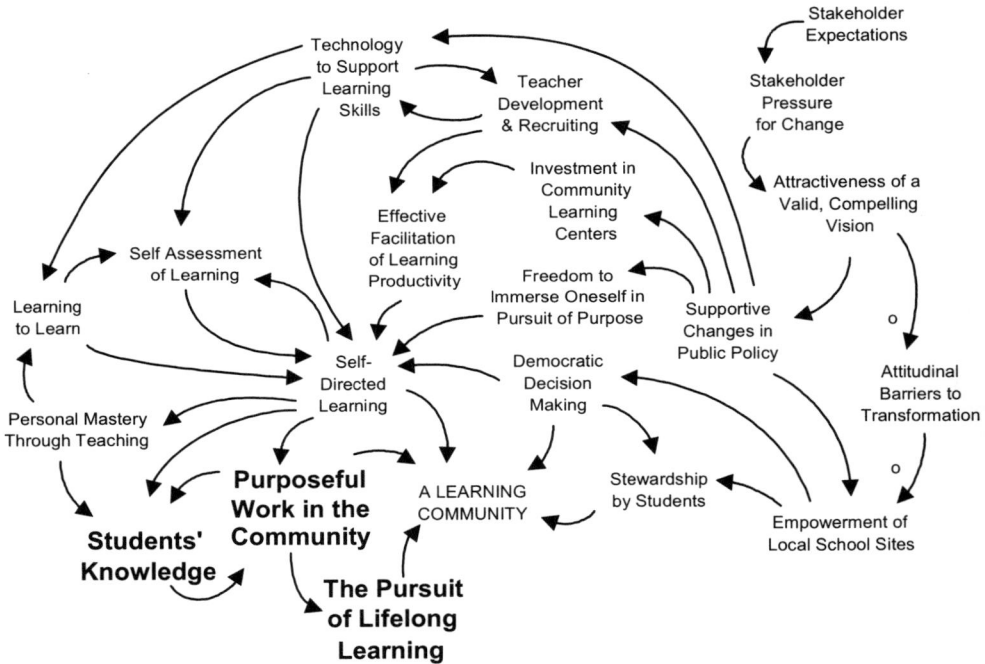

In **Chart 15,** we introduce another – the fourth – important attribute of the learning community: the doing of ***Purposeful Work in the Community***. The successful experiences achieved by older students as they learn, and as they help others in their school to learn, will become known to others outside the school. Leaders of community projects would seek out students to participate in the performance of socially important work that would offer excellent opportunities to apply ***Students' Knowledge*** and to interface with adults and responsible leaders. As students demonstrated success in their "apprenticeships" to the schools and community work, they and school leadership would find many new opportunities to form high-quality apprenticeships and internships with business and nonprofit organizations. In fact, with flexible scheduling options, students in the pursuit of self-directed learning could use their own initiative in creating such opportunities.

The schools we create that will offer effective Learning for the 21st Century will promote the ***Pursuit of Lifelong Learning,*** the fifth key characteristic of the Learning Community we aspire toward.

Many attitudinal and structural changes will have to occur, but students in our new schools will become free to utilize the learning environment as they choose in order to complete projects and work on the individual programs they have formalized with their learning facilitators. A demand will emerge for these open learning environments to be made available to learners of all ages, including parents, worker re-trainees, and anyone engaged in lifelong learning.

Developments of this nature will have a potentially dramatic impact on many colleges, as they exist today. Many will link up with local school districts to extend their services to elementary and secondary schools. Many leading universities will go global, and for-profit universities will grow in importance, particularly as providers of continuous, lifelong learning.

The foundation concept for the development of this theory, thus far, has been the strong conviction that each individual student, when engaged in the right educational structure, can learn and can, thereby, achieve success in school. However, we

Chart 16: Schools must become Learning Organizations.

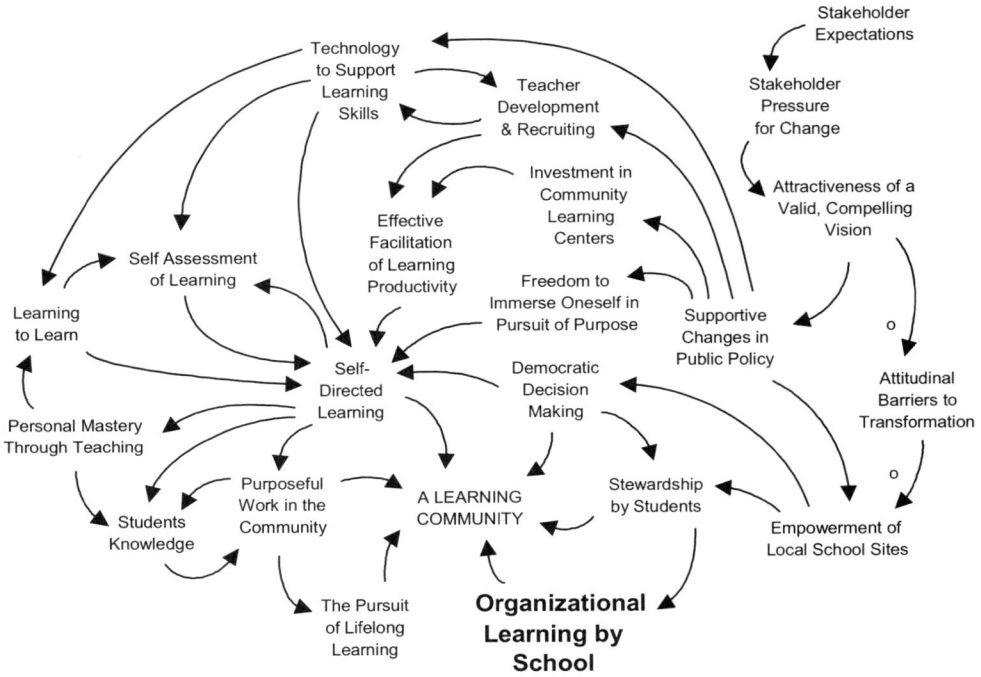

recognize that schools, themselves, are capable of learning; that they – like other organizations of the Information Age – must become learning organizations. These schools would constantly adapt themselves to the needs of students and continuously improve their own methods based on their members' collective experiences and increasing awareness of the Global Best Practices.

The sixth essential characteristic of a learning community, also mapped in **Chart 16,** is *Organizational Learning by the School.*

In addition to increasing the awareness of what is possible, another one of the powerful influences propelling a school toward becoming a learning organization is the sense of stewardship by older students who feel accountable for the long-term success of newly entering younger students. As we have pointed out earlier, this sense of responsibility follows from an effective, democratic governance process that involves students in meaningful ways in collaborative decision making. Also, students who take on the responsibility for assessing school performance create a wonderful learning opportunity.

But, of course, teachers must also be involved in a long-term commitment to the school and to increasing the scope of their contributions to school and student success. An important dimension of organizational learning by the school is teacher development in such areas as Total Quality, cooperative learning and technology.

But even beyond that, schools need to better evaluate their own success at creating and sustaining the factors that are necessary for student achievement. Schools, too, need to develop an effective performance measurement capability. The performance goals for the schools and other components of the whole education system would, in effect, quantify the vision. As we have seen in business, the development and implementation of a performance goal and measurement process is essential for driving the transformation of an organization. The "power of the performance gap" generates the leverage that makes real change possible.

Chart 17: Business Support and Expertise for Achieving Change is a powerful variable in the system. It influences the Empowerment of Local School Sites, Organizational Learning by the School, and the Pursuit of Lifelong Learning. Business Support arises from an Attractive, Compelling Vision.

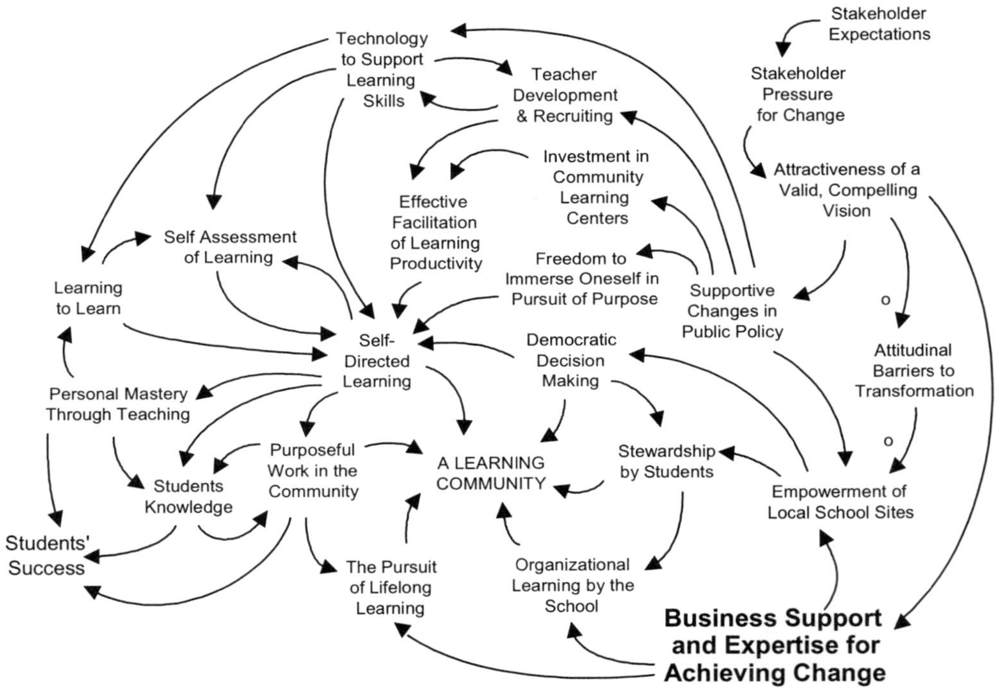

A very useful performance assessment model for schools and other educational system components would draw upon Wisdom Dynamics' Dynamic Scoring™, which is based on the principles of systems thinking and system dynamics. Suitable for all industries, this new accounting model does more than measure inputs and outputs. Instead, it creates a dynamic picture of how the organization works to create value, revealing the feedback structures and patterns of behavior that produce results. It then quantifies the relationships of all key variables in a computer model that can be used for scenario planning and simulation of alternative strategies, so that they can be tested before they are applied. The "systems map" we are developing, illustrates a systemic structure that could be used to launch such a strategic simulation.

An increasing number of the world's leading business organizations are driving hard to become effective learning organizations and creators of knowledge that generate value for their customers or clients. They view it as a matter of survival. It does mean, however, that their future depends on recruiting and challenging employees who are skilled learners. It is, therefore, in the vital interest of business to engage directly in the transformation of education to meet the needs of the 21st century. Right now, the strong commitment that many businesses have made to becoming learning organizations, and to improving public education, means that *Business Support and Expertise for Achieving Change,* shown in **Chart 17,** could be another powerful enabler for organizational learning by schools.

Business support for seeking change in our schools does not, however, come easily. As with any other stakeholder in a complex social or economic system, the business community requires an attractive, valid, and compelling vision for the future – one that promises lasting benefits for itself, as well as for the others. When those future benefits become apparent, then businesses will become eager and active participants in the mission of transforming education, including support to empower local school district sites in their pursuit to achieve the vision of the learning community.

Chart 18: The complex system described here is designed to deliver three outcomes: greater Students' Success, greater Equity for Our Students, and Higher Quality at Lower Cost.

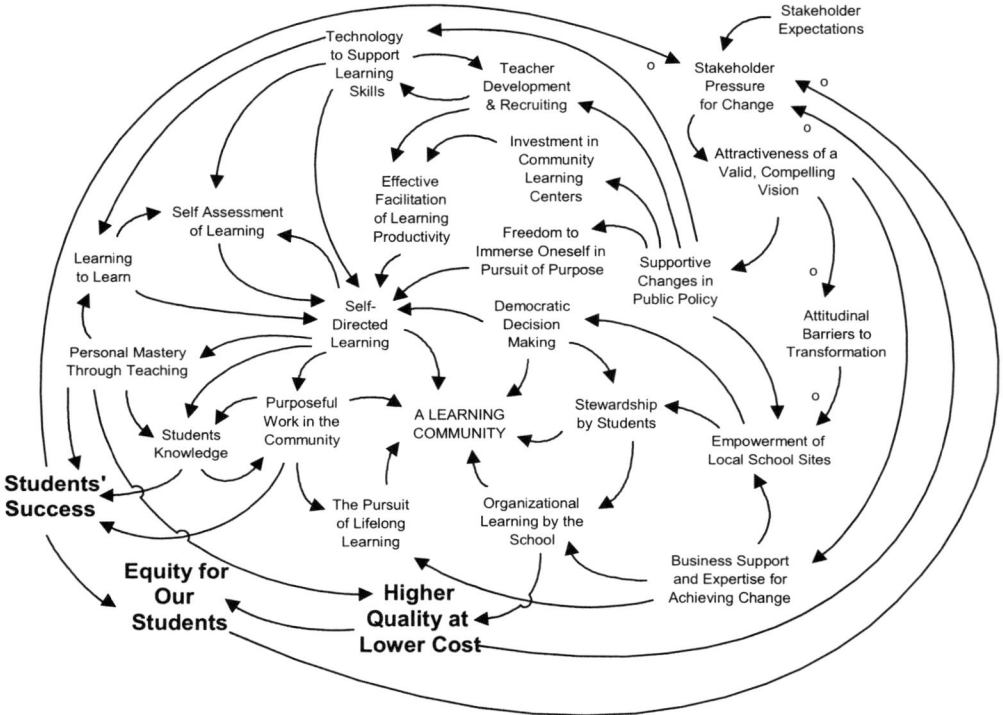

Business possesses skills in managing innovation, research and development, technology, and change enablement, which are scarce within the education community. Business should redirect some of their support of traditional programs toward fundamental change by facilitating community visioning and building prototypes of new schools. Once the new schools are in operation, community pressure for rapid conversion to the new education system will follow.

Another concrete way that a business can support the learning community is to promote the concept and practice of lifelong learning for its employees and to seek assistance from learning institutions for that purpose.

What has been described thus far is, indeed, a complex system. In fact, the variables shown are just a small number of the many interacting factors that are really involved. However, these are the most important relationships affecting *Students' Success*. This is perhaps the ultimate purpose of the efforts we make, and the first of the three stakeholder expectations identified earlier.

As is shown in **Chart 18**, there are many factors that, either directly or indirectly, affect student success. Most directly are the achievement of personal mastery of learning and the capability to do purposeful work within the community.

While success in school for each individual student is an overarching aim of the effort to transform education, there are other important and related objectives, too. In order to sustain the resources necessary to accelerate the pace and scope of student success, our education system needs to perform at *Higher Quality at Lower Cost*. This is the second of the three most significant stakeholder expectations described earlier. The progress we make to improve the pace and quality of student success, while simultaneously lowering the cost and improving the quality of our education system will have a profound effect on society. That effect will be to substantially increase the level of *Equity for Our Students.*

As members of democratic societies who have deep commitments to, and reverence for, human rights, the pursuit of equity for all of our children is of paramount importance for us all. Equity for our students is the third major stakeholder expectation discussed earlier.

Chart 19: Stakeholder Expectations, in this system, is the only endogenous variable, which means that it is not influenced by any other variable "within" the system. As such, it is perhaps the most powerful driver for transforming education. Certainly, without enduring Stakeholder Expectations for a dramatically more productive system, no positive change will occur.

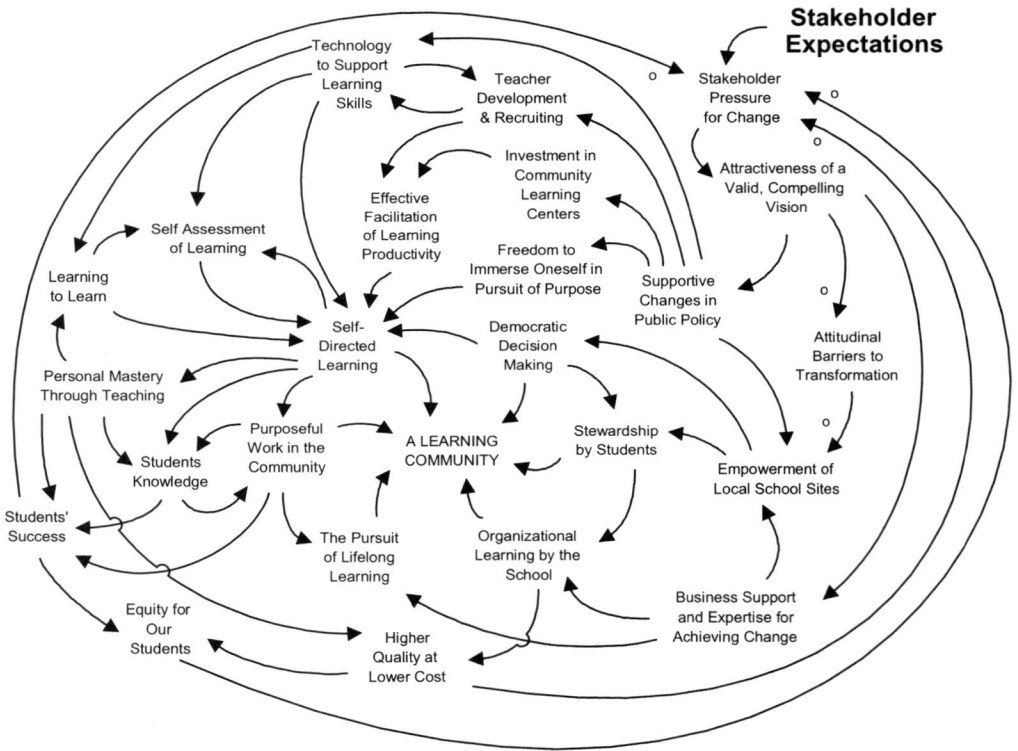

We are nearing the end of our journey on this pathway through the complex system that will transform education. Yet, as we examine the structural diagram of this system in **Chart 19**, it is important that we acknowledge the feedback relationships that are the source of dynamic behavior.

Because student success in school is one of the major shared *Stakeholder Expectations* and because many stakeholders believe it is currently lower than it should be, there is considerable pressure from stakeholders for change that will increase student success. This causal relationship is represented by the link from students' success to stakeholder pressure for change. Note the "o" at the head of that arrow. It means that as student success goes up, the pressure from stakeholders will tend to decrease because the expectation for success is being met. But note, too, that student success will result from the complex feedback connections that are set in motion by the amount of stakeholder pressure for change that exists now.

Increasing student success alone is not sufficient. Those results must be achieved at reasonable cost. And with increasing awareness of cost/benefit relationships revealed by international comparisons, "reasonable cost" will mean "lower cost" for industrial nations, who can use technology, self-directed learning and reconfigured classes to achieve productivity gains. Developing nations will face rising costs, to incorporate modern technology, however, they will avoid the wasteful alternative of copying the obsolete Industrial Age model.

And, finally, almost all of us share the inspiring dream of equality of educational opportunity for all of the students within our communities. This aspiration is an important stakeholder expectation. And, until there is a major increase in equity for our students, this expectation will not be satisfied, and the pressure for change will remain strong. We believe this will create a strong demand for business-sponsored community learning centers for employees' children, the intent for which will be to supplement everyone's school experience. These developments would provide additional pressures and examples for educational change. In a world of increasing complexity and interdependency, we must all strive to understand and master the systemic forces that are at work in our environment in which public education plays such an important role.

Chart 20: Stakeholder Expectations, in this system, are per-haps the most powerful drivers for transforming education.   The three high leverage interventions for achieving Stakeholder Expectations are Self-Directed Learning, the Attractiveness of a Valid, Compelling Vision, and Business Support and Expertise for Achieving Change.

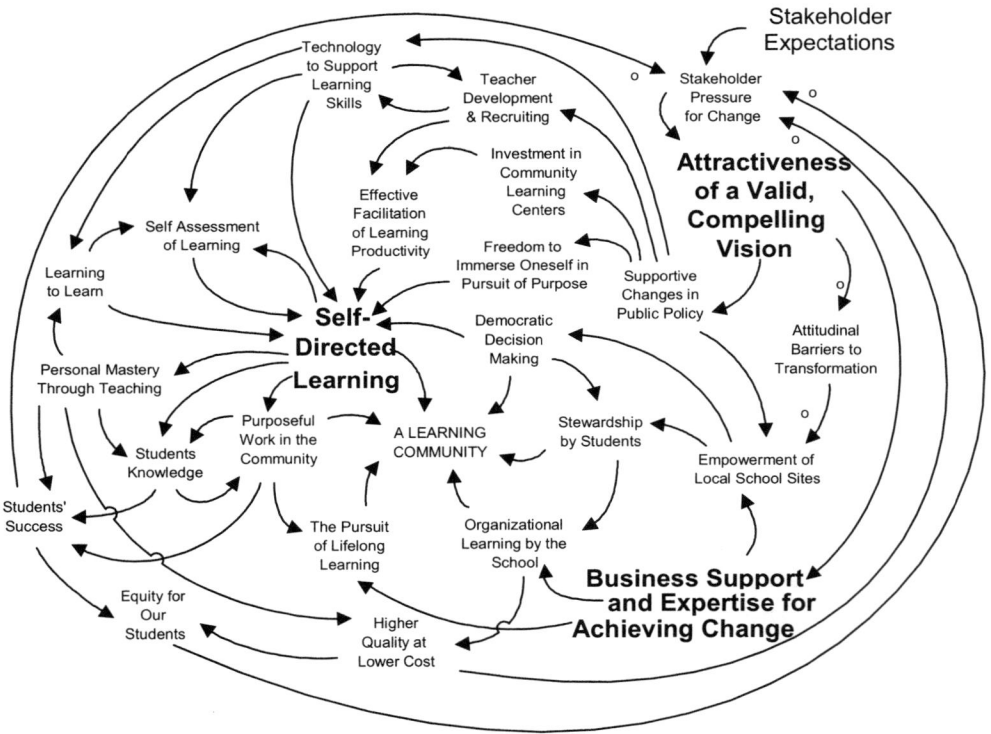

All of us must be fully engaged stakeholders in efforts everywhere to transform education. There are three especially high leverage interventions, shown in **Chart 20** of our systems map, for achieving *Stakeholder Expectations*.

The first is **Self-Directed Learning**. This directly addresses the empowerment of our students to more effectively discover and enjoy the pursuit of knowledge.

The second is the **Attractiveness of a Valid, Compelling Vision**. This is necessary to convert the power of stakeholder pressure for change into concrete, vivid images of the benefits that change will deliver.

The third is **Business Support and Expertise for Achieving Change**. Businesses in the brain-powered economy of the Information Age have been transforming themselves from the Industrial Age for a decade or more. They have learned much that can be effectively shared with the players in our educational systems. All three high leverage interventions are highlighted in Chart 20.

The transformation of education from a mechanistic system to a living, "learning system," in which youngsters learn to interact with adults in the meaningful work of influencing the learning community, knows no boundaries. Linkages of individuals and learning communities will be formed, leading to a global community of learners. In transforming our schools into a learning system, we are creating opportunities for young people from all countries of the world to work together and to forge friendships and interdependencies that will create a global community of learners, providing us with the capacity to anticipate and address global challenges relating to the economy, the environment, public health, and world peace.

APPENDIX F

ASSESSING SCHOOL PERFORMANCE

This appendix suggests potential performance measures associated with each of the key variables introduced and described in Appendix E. The words or phrases below each key variable suggest performance indicators that can be measured over time. The establishment and monitoring of quantifiable measures will enable us to detect if we are approaching or exceeding the goals we establish for factors that are important to us.

The creation of a "Performance Goals and Measurement Capability" is essential for the process of actually achieving a vision for the future of education. The transformation of education depends on the "power of the performance gap," whereby the tension between the goal and actual condition for an important factor becomes one of the driving forces for change.

Imagine the immense power for transformation that could exist if all the forces for change are working in the same direction. However, now imagine the "gridlock" that could occur if the forces for change are seeking opposite or intersecting directions!

Therefore, effective change management requires that performance goals and measurements be aligned with the strategy and purpose of the process, organization, or whole system that is to be changed.

The learners, involved in the design of the learning process and all decisions that affect them, should perform the purposeful work necessary to gather the data to maintain the school's performance measurement system. This will deepen their understanding of how the world works and how their school works, while reinforcing their sense of personal responsibility. This integration of accountability with learning stands in sharp contrast to the current debate over standards and testing in which traditional schools are requiring more tests of passive students.

Following, then, are suggested performance measures for each of these key variables:

A Learning Community
- Stakeholder satisfaction with the community's learning capability
- Demand for admittance to the school
- Level of parent participation
- Warmth of a close-knit community

Self-Directed Learning
- Number of students in individualized learning plans
- Fraction of school time spent in discovery learning

Democratic Decision making
- Frequency of voting on operating policies
- Quality of democratic structures
- Self-initiated conflict resolution

Stewardship by Students for Their Schools
- Time lost to student discipline
- Fraction of student time in service to the school and other students
- Fraction of student time engaged in assessing and reporting on their school's performance

Empowerment of Local School Sites
- Authority level of a single school to implement change
- Cash flow

Supportive Changes in Public Policy
- The government's willingness to fund diverse innovation.
- Public policies that enable self-directed learning

Attitudinal Barriers to Transformation
- Stakeholders' comfort level with current conditions

Stakeholder Expectations
- Clarity of stakeholder expectations
- Usefulness of stakeholder goals for school performance
- Parent satisfaction

- Learner satisfaction

Stakeholder Pressure for Change
- Stakeholders' level of passion to change the status quo
- Size of performance gaps to performance goals

Attractiveness of a Valid, Compelling Vision
- Stakeholders' enthusiasm for the Shared Vision
- Clarity of Purpose and Vision for the school

Freedom to Immerse Oneself in Pursuit of Purpose
- Fraction of students' time in fragmented schedules
- Fun and joy of learning

Technology to Support Learning
- Number of students with access to learning technologies
- Quality of technology resources

Teacher Development and Recruiting
- Fraction of all teachers who are "qualified" as Learning Productivity Facilitators
- Fraction of new-hire teachers who are trained and qualified as Learning Productivity Facilitators
- Facilitator productivity

Self-Assessment of Learning
- Fraction of students performing self-assessment on a continuous basis

Learning-to-Learn
- Number and scope of formal learning-to-learn programs
- Fraction of students' time in formal learning-to-learn training programs

Effective Facilitation of Learning Productivity
- Scores on Performance Rubrics measuring learning-to-learn skills
- Positive change in learning productivity measures, i.e., knowledge units added per student, per year, per time unit of effort by learners and/or teachers

Investment in Community Learning Centers
- Number of community learning center sites delivering School-of-the-Future learning opportunities.
- Fraction of community members who participate in CLC learning opportunities or programs.

Personal Mastery Through Teaching
- Fraction of students' time sharing knowledge with others
- Number of students with older student mentors

Purposeful Work in the Community
- Number of students in productive "Apprenticeships for Students"
- Degree of student participation in community leadership roles

The Pursuit of Lifelong Learning
- Number of schools offering lifelong learning programs

Organizational Learning by the School
- Clarity of a Shared Vision for the school
- Fraction of teachers' time in team learning and dialogue
- Degree of alignment to the school's "theory of success"
- Clarity of goals and performance measurements

Business Support and Expertise for Achieving Change
- Number of schools in alliances with businesses
- Clarity of business expectations for students
- Fraction of businesspersons' time with students in self-directed learning programs

Students' Knowledge
- Ratio of accumulated knowledge units gained per student vs. "average" of same measure in other schools.
- Scores on academic achievement tests at graduation time
- Fraction of the students' knowledge units achieved that are highly valued by community employers and civic leaders

- Fraction of knowledge units achieved categorized as "college level" material.

Student Success
- Dropout rate
- Graduation rate
- Peer recognition for learning skills
- Number of students doing purposeful work
- Number of students with mastery certificates
- College acceptances
- Number and quality of projects
- Accomplishments of graduates

Higher Quality at Lower Cost
- Education costs per student
- Ratio of value-added time to non-value-added time in school

Equity for Our Students
- Number of students with common, Vision-based expectations for success
- Fraction of teachers committed to every student
- Fraction of students in tracks

BIBLIOGRAPHY

Ackoff, Russell L. *The Democratic Corporation.* Oxford University Press, 1994.

Berryman, Sue E., and Thomas R. Bailey. *The Double Helix of Education and the Economy.* The Institute on Education and the Economy, 1992.

Brooks, Jacqueline G., and Martin G. Brooks. *The Case for Constructivist Classrooms.* Association for Supervision and Curriculum Development, 1993.

Caine, Renata Nummela and Geoffrey Caine. *Education on the Edge of Possibility.* Association for Supervision and Curriculum Development, 1997.

Chubb, John E. and Terry M. Moe. *Politics, Markets & Americas Schools.* The Brookings Institution, 1990.

Dewey, John J. *The School and Society.* Southern Illinois University Press, 1976.
          Democracy and Education. New York: The Free Press, 1944.
          Essays on Education and Politics: The Middle Works (1899-1924) Southern Illinois University Press, 1985.

Drucker, Peter F. *Post-Capitalist Society.* Harper Collins, 1993.
          Management Challenges for the 21st Century. HarperCollins, 1999.

Eccles, J.C. *Evolution of the Brain: Creation of the Self.* London:Routledge, 1989.

Edwards, Carolyn, and Lella Gandini, and George Forman. *The Hundred Languages of Children: The Reggio Emilia Approach to Early Childhood Education.* Ablex Publishing, 1993.

Franklin, Benjamin. *Franklin: The Autobiography.* Vintage Books, 1990.

Forrester, Jay W. *Collected Papers of Jay W. Forrester.* Wright-Allen Press, 1975
          Urban Dynamics. Productivity Press, 1969.

Friedman, Milton & Rose. *Free to Choose.* Harcourt Brace & Company 1980.

Gardner, Howard. *Frames of Mind: The Theory of Multiple Intelligences.* Basic Books, 1983.

Goodlad, John I. and Timothy J. McMannon. *The Public Purpose of Education an Schooling.* Jossey-Bass, 1997.

Greenberg, Daniel. *A Clearer View: New Insights into the Sudbury Valley School.* The Sudbury Valley School Press, 2000.

Handy, Charles B. *The Age of Unreason.* Harvard Business School Press, 1989.

Keller, Helen. *The Story of my Life.* Bantam Books, 1990.

Kuhn, Thomas S. *The Structure of Scientific Revolutions.* 2nd ed. The University of Chicago Press, 1970.

Papert, Seymour. *Mindstorms: Children, Computers and Powerful Ideas.* Basic Books, 1980.

Perelman, Lewis J. *School's Out: Hyperlearning, The New Technology and The End of Education.* Morrow, 1992.

Senge, Peter M. *The Fifth Discipline: The Art and Practice of the Learning Organization.* Doubleday/Currency, 1990.
_____ *Schools That Learn.* Doubleday/Currency, 2000.

Vygotsky, L.S. *Mind in Society.* Harvard University Press, 1978.

Wheatley, M.J. *Leadership and the New Science: Learning About Organization from an Orderly Universe.* Berrett-Koehler, 1992.

Dialogue with the author

Your comments and questions may be directed to Morton Egol at mortonegol@wisdomdynamics.com.